T5-AFY-409

THE GARDEN LIBRARY

HERBS

THE GARDEN LIBRARY

HERBS

Kenneth A. Beckett

BALLANTINE BOOKS · NEW YORK

Editor
Anthony Livesey

Designers
Julia Harris
Jane Owen

Managing Editor
Jackie Douglas

Art Director
Roger Bristow

Consultants
Margaret McQuade Hagedorn
James Fanning

Published in Great Britain in 1984 by
Dorling Kindersley Limited

The Garden Library HERBS was conceived,
edited and designed by Dorling Kindersley Limited,
9 Henrietta Street, London WC2E 8PS

Copyright © 1984 by Dorling Kindersley Limited

All rights reserved under International and Pan-American
Conventions. Published in the United States by
Ballantine Books, a division of Random House,
Inc., New York, and simultaneously in
Canada by Random House of Canada
Limited, Toronto

Library of Congress Catalog Card Number: 83-91159

ISBN 0-345-33662-3

Manufactured in the United States of America

First Ballantine Books Trade Edition: April 1984
10 9 8 7 6 5 4 3 2

Contents

Care and cultivation

For most people, herbs are plants solely used to flavor food. In the past it was the medicinal qualities of a herb that were valued, the knowledge of which was gained by trial and error over a long period of human history. In the strict botanical sense, a herb is any plant that is soft or non-woody, such as herbaceous annuals, biennials and perennials. Many vegetables and salad plants come into this category and were formerly known as pot herbs.

Recently there has been a resurgence of interest in both culinary and medicinal herbs and it is with these that this book is concerned. There are a number of reasons for this renewed interest, including reaction to the bland, processed foods so generally on offer, and scepticism about modern, synthesized drugs, which can have alarming side effects. Much though man depends on, and even enjoys, his highly civilized existence, the more he is cut off from the natural world the more he seems to yearn for it. Hence the upsurge of interest in gardening, health foods and herbal remedies.

This book is essentially a horticultural guide, illustrating and describing plants and giving cultural information for a selection of the best known kinds. Only their main culinary and medicinal values are mentioned, for how to use herbs for these purposes is the province of cookery experts and herbal medicine practitioners. Medicinal herbs in particular must be prepared and used by an expert, or under guidance from one, for some can be dangerous if the correct dose is exceeded.

In ancient times, herbs were gathered in the wild by those members of a community with the necessary knowledge. Later, when man lived a more settled existence, herbs were grown together with staple food plants. Special plots were set aside for herbs as long ago as the ancient civilizations of China, Persia (Iran), Greece and Rome. Gradually, mixed with plants grown purely for their beauty, these plots became the progenitors of our modern gardens, tended entirely for esthetic reasons.

Many herb plants are not only useful but are visually attractive or fragrant and a bed or corner devoted to them can be an appealing garden feature. Once these beds had very formal bounds, usually geometrical in shape, sometimes edged with box (boxwood) hedging, trimmed down to 1 ft (30 cm) tall or below. Less rigid designs evolved later but a formal approach is still popular.

If more than half a dozen different sorts of herb are to be grown, it is worthwhile making a feature

These 17th-century formal designs, in patterns resembling complicated knots, look best in large gardens for they need an area not less than 10 × 8 ft (3 × 2.4 m) and preferably larger. Rake the area level, then carefully measure the main points of the design and mark with canes. Draw the design outline with a pointed stick and, to enhance the period atmosphere, plant this surround with boxwood.

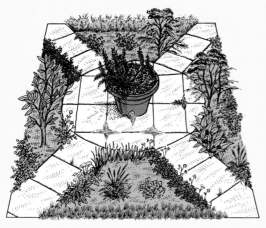

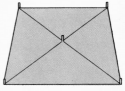

This design (left), approximately 6 ft (1.8 m) square, is ideal for a small garden. Make sure the site is level and mark out the square (above) with pegs and string.

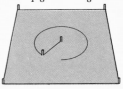

Mark out the central 3 ft (90 cm) wide circular area, using two pegs and an 18 in (45 cm) length of string or twine. Lay the paths, using paving slabs 1 ft (30 cm) square; then plant the garden.

of them. A paved area of gray stone or concrete makes a good background and provides clean, dry access at all times. A checkerboard pattern can be adopted, flagstones alternating with open soil squares for the plants. Alternatively, a square, oblong, circular or other geometrically-shaped bed can be made in the center or to one side of a patio or similar paved area. If large enough, the bed should be bisected with small, paved access paths and be either at ground level or raised. Raised beds add a new dimension to the garden and are helpful to gardeners with back trouble. As a change from stone or concrete, red bricks or tiles can be used but they need greater skill in laying well and if done by a contractor are expensive.

If there is little garden space, a wide variety of containers can be used, from pots to window-boxes, tubs and troughs. There are a number of advantages to this method of growing herbs. The containers can be sited within easy reach of the kitchen door; soil preference can be observed, for example moist and rich soil for mint, poor, sandier soil for thyme. Herbs needing shade can be placed in the shadow of a nearby tree or building. Half-hardy herbs, such as rosemary and sweet bay, can be easily moved in severe winter conditions to a shed or greenhouse without root disturbance. Invasive herbs, such as the mints, can be confined in containers and prevented from becoming a nuisance.

Soil

In general, herbs are easily grown and are tolerant of poor conditions. A surprising number are native to the Mediterranean region, where they inhabit dry, relatively poor and often stony soils. There are, of course, exceptions. Mint and lovage thrive

Well-decayed farmyard manure, garden compost, peat moss or leaf-mold are essential to the fertility of soil and health of plants. It is best lightly forked into the top 6–10 in (15–25 cm) of earth but can be left, evenly spread, as a surface mulch.

On poorer soils, an annual dressing of general fertilizer is advisable. Spread this evenly, giving the amount recommended by the manufacturers, and rake into the soil surface. The best time to do this is just before planting or sowing.

in moist, rich land, but even plants of this sort are reasonably tolerant.

Although herbs are fairly adaptable plants, this is no reason to be totally complacent about the soil they are to occupy. Basically, it should be of moderate fertility and well drained. Very sandy or thin, limy soils should be enriched with organic matter, which is the basis of all soil fertility and provides the essential humus — a complex colloid which coats soil particles and holds water and dissolved mineral salts. Organic matter comes in a variety of guises, including peat moss, farmyard or stable manure, garden compost and leaf-mold. Spread a layer at least 2 in (5 cm) deep on the soil surface, then lightly fork into the top spit. This is best done during the fall to spring period. Later, just before planting or sowing, apply a light dressing of general fertilizer and rake into the surface. One of the slow release granular fertilizers is recommended.

Soil for containers
Soil for pots and other containers should be a little richer than that in the garden, for in a pot the root system of a plant is restricted to a very small volume of soil, much less than it would have in a bed or border. A commercial soil or loam-based potting mix is usually satisfactory. The all-peat mixes should have one-quarter to one-third part by volume of coarse sand or grit added. This adds weight, allows more ready penetration of water when the peat dries out and makes it more acceptable to the roots of such Mediterrean herbs as rosemary, sage and thyme. As an alternative, ordinary garden soil can be used but it must be enriched with at least one-third part by volume of well rotted organic matter, plus a good fertilizer, ideally a slow-release type. To each bushel of basic soil mix, add 6 oz (165 gm) of fertilizer and an equal amount of lime. If the basic soil is known to be alkaline, the extra lime can be left out. (A bushel measure is based upon a box with the dimensions 22 × 10 × 10 in, 55 × 25 × 25 cm.) However good this potting mixture is, vigorous plants will soon use up the main minerals and supplementary feeding is advisable. This is best given as a commercial liquid feed, used to the makers' instructions. Feeding should start about eight weeks after the final planting or potting.

Situation
Most herbs need plenty of sun, so the position of these plants should be as sunny as possible. However, the majority will tolerate sites where the sun shines for up to half of each day only. They will not

be of the high quality of those grown in full sun but good enough for most culinary and medicinal purposes. There are herbs that will tolerate more than half day shade, for example mint, angelica, feverfew, lovage, horseradish, sweet cicely and woodruff. In areas where summers are often cool and cloudy, the sunniest site should be chosen. In sunnier climes, a shady site is acceptable.

Planting

Young herb plants are usually bought in containers. Watered thoroughly and removed from their pots with care, they should be planted out in their permanent sites at any time from spring onward. In mild winter areas, where frosts are slight or at least short lived, planting can take place through the winter as well. Plants dug from the open ground, and especially divisions with little or no soil adhering to the roots, are best dealt with only while dormant, that is from fall through late spring.

Dibber

Trowel

A trowel is usually the best tool for planting. Remove the plants from their containers and lay them out where they are to be planted. Dig a hole a little larger than the root ball and put the plant into position a fraction lower than it was in the container; then fill in all round and firm with the fists. Unless the soil is already thoroughly moist, it is advisable to water each plant well to settle it in and aid root establishment.

Small plants can be set out with a dibber but for most herbs a trowel is a better tool. Dig the hole larger than the plant's root ball.

Loosen soil at the bottom of the hole if it seems compacted. Set the plant in the hole so that the root ball is just below the soil level.

Fill around the root ball with loose soil and firm with the fists.

In many instances, a single plant of any one herb is all that is needed. Where more than one is required, as with such annuals as caraway, coriander and dill, they must be spaced sufficiently far apart to allow full development. As a rule of thumb guide, a suitable distance apart is that equal to half the ultimate height of a mature plant. Tall, thin species can be set closer than this, wide spreading ones farther apart.

Aftercare

Once planting is completed, the maintenance of a herb garden is primarily a matter of weeding and watering in dry spells of those species that need a regular supply of moisture. Examples include mints, angelica and lovage. Unless a plant is grown for its seeds, it is advisable to remove spent flower heads and even the flowering stems while young to promote plenty of fresh leaves.

In areas of severe winters, particularly in northern New England, a number of herbs cannot survive. These include sweet bay, rosemary, lemon verbena, lemon and common thyme and sweet geranium; all must be given winter protection. When a plant is reasonably hardy, such as common thyme, a light mulch of hay or bracken fern, or a cloche, is often sufficient. Alternatively, the plant can be lifted or cuttings rooted and kept in a greenhouse or by a sunny window in the home. Even hardy evergreen herbs can be dealt with in this way, to provide fresh leaves or shoots in winter. Young plants, particularly rooted cuttings, may get rather thin and drawn in the poor winter light and will need the tips pinched out to encourage bushiness. Herbs such as thyme and sage are apt to get leggy over the years and are best sheared over each spring or in late summer in mild winter areas.

Most of the more shrubby or woody-based herbs, such as hyssop, sage, thyme, rue and lemon verbena, tend to become leggy after the first few years. Cut these back after flowering or in spring to maintain bushy growth.

Propagation

All the herbs mentioned in this book are easily propagated by either seeds, cuttings or division. Depending on the species of plant, one or other method of propagation is usually to be preferred and this information is given for each herb between pages 18 and 94.

SEED All true annual herbs, such as anise, coriander and dill, can be raised only from seed. It is also usual to raise some of the tender perennials annually from seed, examples including basil and sweet marjoram. The seed of other herbs is generally available and provides a very satisfying way of starting a herb collection.

There are two ways of raising herbs from seed: sowing on site (in the ground where the plants are to grow and mature) or in pots under glass or in the home. The latter method is used for species that are frost tender or need a long growing season.

SOWING UNDER COVER As only small numbers of plants are needed, small pots or pans make suitable seed sowing containers: 3–4 in (7.5–10 cm) are useful sizes. It is best to use a sterile seed-sowing mix to make sure there are no weed seeds or pest

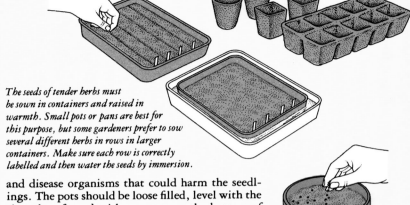

The seeds of tender herbs must be sown in containers and raised in warmth. Small pots or pans are best for this purpose, but some gardeners prefer to sow several different herbs in rows in larger containers. Make sure each row is correctly labelled and then water the seeds by immersion.

and disease organisms that could harm the seedlings. The pots should be loose filled, level with the rim, then firmed with a presser or the bottom of another pot. Leave a gap of ½–¾ in (1–2 cm) between the rim and soil surface. Drainage material is not required in small pots and pans. The seeds must be sown thinly, as over-crowded seedlings are prone to damping-off disease. Very small seeds can be difficult to spread thinly and evenly. To overcome this, mix them with several volumes of fine, dry sand and sow the mixture as seed. If they are large enough to handle with the fingers or with tweezers, there is much to be said for space sowing – that is, setting the seeds ½–1½ in (1–4 cm) apart each way. This saves pricking off the subsequent seedlings. The actual distance apart will depend on the seed size and vigor of the seedling. For example, borage must be placed at 1½ in (4 cm), sage at ¾ in (2 cm) and feverfew at ½ in (1 cm) apart. When sown, they should be covered with a layer of seed-sowing mix equal in thickness to the largest diameter of the seed concerned. The pots must then be watered either by immersion or with a watering can with a fine spray nozzle. The immersion method is always to be preferred for very small seeds.

Once the pots have drained, place them in a propagating case or on a greenhouse bench or indoor window-ledge. Excepting those placed in a propagating case, the sown containers should be put in a plastic bag or covered with a sheet of glass. This prevents rapid drying of the soil surface during the critical germination period. A suitable minimum temperature is warm (around 60°F, 16°C), though for the more tropical species, such as cumin or peppers, 65–70°F (18–20°C) is best. Optimum germination temperatures are mentioned, when relevant, in the descriptions of individual herbs that follow. Over-high temperatures

If only a few plants are required, it is best to space-sow the seeds in small pots or pans (top). Use tweezers for the larger seeds. After covering with seed-sowing mix, place the pots in a propagating case or a plastic bag (above). As soon as the seedlings are large enough to handle, prick them off into larger containers (below) to avoid overcrowding.

can be damaging and even inhibit germination. For this reason, the glass- or plastic-covered seed pots must not be stood in direct sunlight. If a shady position cannot be found, they should be covered with a single sheet of newspaper. After the first three to five days, the containers must be looked at regularly for germination and excess condensation removed. Once the seedlings have sprouted, remove the covering and place the container in good light. For the first few days they must be screened from direct hot sunlight, which could shrivel emerging seedlings. It is important to foster sturdy, short jointed young plants, so later they must be given as much light as they will take. Few herb seedlings need shading once their first leaves are fully expanded. If they bend towards the light, it is advisable to put them nearer to the glass and to turn them daily to maintain straight growth.

PRICKING OFF As soon as the seed leaves are fully expanded and the first true, or rough, leaf shows, it is time for spacing out or pricking off. The pot of seedlings should be knocked out in a block and the contents gently shaken apart. Fill larger containers with potting mix and plant the seedlings 1½–2 in (4–5 cm) apart. Use a dibber or widger to make the holes. Each seedling must then be set a little deeper than in the seed pot and gently firmed. After watering with a fine-rosed can, return them to the same growing conditions.

Annual herbs being raised for the open garden can be left in these larger containers until planting out time. Those intended as pot plants need to be placed in single containers. As a guide, once the leaves of the young plants touch and start to overlap it is time to pot. An average container size for this initial potting is 3 in (7.5 cm).

SOWING ON SITE Hardy annual and biennial herbs are best sown on site. Previously prepared soil should be lightly firmed by treading, then raked level. Areas alloted to each species can then be marked out with a pointed stick. Each area should be sown either in a series of short parallel drills or broadcast. The drills must be shallow, no more than ¼ in (6 mm) deep for fine seeds. A piece of straight board and a pointed stick are the best tools for the job.

The easiest way to make a neat seed drill of the required depth is to use a length of straight board and a strong, pointed stick or corner of a hoe.

Broadcast sowing, then raking the seeds into the surface, is easier but can be more wasteful of seed. When the seedlings show true or rough leaves, they must be thinned, the unwanted ones being pulled out carefully so as not to disturb those that remain. A first thinning can be 2 in (5 cm) apart, leaving the final spacing until several weeks later. If dry weather follows, watering is advisable.

CUTTINGS Many herbs can be increased from cuttings in either spring, late summer or, less usually, in fall. Cuttings are short lengths of stem. Young leafy shoots are known as softwood cuttings; those a little older that are beginning to get woody at the base are semi-hardwood. Fully mature woody stems, which may be leafless when taken in fall, are known as hardwood. Softwood cuttings are usually stem tips or whole shoots, 2–4 in (5–10 cm) in length. Sever each one cleanly with a sharp knife or razor blade just beneath a leaf joint (node). The leaves from the lower half must then be cut, nipped or pulled off and the base dipped in a combined rooting powder and fungicide mixture. An ideal rooting mix is a 50/50 mixture of peat moss and coarse sand, fine grit or perlite. Softwood cuttings need a propagating case or plastic bag and a warm temperature of at least 60–65°F (16–18°C).

When trimming softwood or semi-hardwood cuttings, lay the chosen stems on a wooden surface and sever with a razor blade or sharp knife (below far left). Immediately the cuttings are trimmed, dip them in rooting powder (below center) and plant in suitable potting mix (below).

Semi-hardwood cuttings can be similarly treated or placed in a cold frame. Hardwood cuttings should be inserted on site or in a nursery row in a sheltered location. Cuttings rooted in containers will need potting as soon as they are well rooted and beginning to grow again.

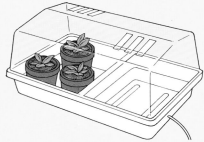

Cuttings taken from most herbs root readily in late summer and early fall. Rooting will be more rapid if the cuttings are placed in a propagator, with gentle bottom heat at about 60–65°F (16–18°C).

Cuttings, and seeds sown in early spring, benefit from extra light, especially during prolonged overcast weather. The small light units made for house plants can be adapted to this use.

Pests and diseases

Happily, most herb plants are remarkably free of pests and diseases, especially if given their preferred cultural requirements for a healthy plant is always less prone to attack by insect pests and fungal diseases. When an attack does occur, it must be dealt with as soon as possible to prevent lasting damage. If chemical sprays or powders are used, they must always be applied according to the makers' instructions. If under-applied an insecticide or fungicide will not be efficient, while over-applied it may damage the plant. Plants so treated must be thoroughly washed after harvesting.

The most likely pests and diseases are given below with their observable symptoms.

Mildly to grossly malformed leaves and stems are usually the result of the feeding habits of piercing and sucking insects. Most commonly seen are the various sorts of aphid or plant lice, also known as greenfly and blackfly. They are tiny, oval-bodied, soft, sometimes winged insects which cluster thickly on the undersides of leaves or on stem tips. They are easily killed with either a contact or systemic insecticide. Limited attacks can be dealt with by squashing between thumb and forefinger or wetting with warm detergent water.

If the deformation of leaves is accompanied by a rather tattered appearance, often with holes of a regular size, then plant bugs are the cause. These are like much larger aphids but fast moving and secretive. The observable damage is the result of much earlier feeding, piercing the tender shoot tips. If this sort of attack occurs regularly, then a preventative series of spray applications should start in late spring.

Stunting and crippling of stems can also be caused by the immature (nymphal) stage of froghoppers and spittlebugs. The latter pest is easily recognized by the spit-like blobs of plant sap

Aphids, or plant lice, can be a nuisance on herb plants of all ages, especially on shoot tips and beneath young leaves. A thorough spraying with an insecticide soon destroys them.

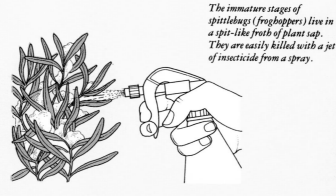

The immature stages of spittlebugs (froghoppers) live in a spit-like froth of plant sap. They are easily killed with a jet of insecticide from a spray.

which shelter the insects. Small infestations can be squashed but larger ones need forceful spraying with an insecticide.

Pieces eaten out of leaf or petal margins usually indicate that caterpillars or earwigs are feeding. Earwigs and some caterpillars hide by day and feed only at night. Where damage is slight, it is worthwhile looking for the pests and dealing with them individually. Larger infestations must be sprayed. Earwigs can be trapped in small pots filled with dry straw, hay or crumpled paper and secured to sticks placed among the plants. These traps must be looked at daily and the pests killed.

Certain herbs, such as sage and garlic, are disinfectants and if dried and sprinkled around plants will protect them from lice and mildew.

Preserving herbs

It is best to use herbs fresh from the plant, but it is also useful to have a supply for the winter and for this stems must be taken in summer and dried.

Leaves with rather ragged holes (above) are often the result of earwigs feeding. More regular holes are likely to be caterpillar damage. Both pests must be destroyed as soon as possible, either by squashing them or spraying with an insecticide.

HARVESTING Leafy stems are best gathered in the morning, as soon as the dew has dried. Although herbs can be cut for use at any time during their active growth, there is a peak time when the essential volatile oils are at their highest. This is the moment to cut and dry them for preserving.

With leafy herbs, the peak period is usually just as the first flowers open. However, for practical purposes cutting can take place from the time when flower heads are first formed until about half have reached the fully open stage. Herbs which do not normally flower, or are prevented from doing so, should be cut the moment a crop of leaves has reached full size. There are some exceptions. For example, chives and parsley can be cut at any time, while sage and Russian tarragon are best gathered before they are fully grown.

Cut off annual herbs near to ground level or where the best leaves start. Perennial sorts must not be cut so hard if further crops are expected; no more than half of the leafy part of each stem should be gathered. If this rule is adhered to, most perennial herbs can be cut two or three times within each growing season. Cut the stems carefully and lay them in trays or shallow baskets. Never store them in sacks and bags or severe bruising will take place, resulting in a loss of volatile oils. If the leaves are splashed with mud they must be washed carefully in tepid water, then gently shaken before preparing for drying.

Flowers to be preserved, such as borage and chamomile, must be handled with extreme care.

Herbs are easily dried by tying the cut stems into small bunches, using five to 10 stems depending on their bushiness (right). Hang these in a warm, airy place. A quicker method is to pick off the leaves and lay them on slatted shelves or frames of chicken wire (below).

Hold them only by their stalks and then lay them in a box or basket no more than one layer deep.

Do not gather fruits and seeds until they are fully mature. The seeds of dill, fennel, anise and caraway, for example, must be fully ripe and part readily from the plant before cutting. Elder-berries must be black-purple before gathering or they will be lacking in flavor and mineral content. As with leaves, fruits and seeds must be washed if they have been splashed with soil. The bruising of soft fruits must be avoided.

Lift roots only when mature in fall, cutting away the leaves and small lateral roots. Very soil encrusted roots must be washed carefully; less dirty ones, usually those from light, sandy ground, can be brushed clean.

DRYING Before the leaves, flowers or seeds can be preserved, they must be dried unless they are to be deep frozen. Drying is the primary means of preservation and, for some herbs at least, is still the best method. The drying must be carried out in the shortest time possible, without actually cooking them. Too much heat is damaging to aroma and causes loss of volatile oil; for this reason herbs must not be dried in direct sunlight. Too little heat and subsequent slow drying, on the other hand, allows some decomposition of leaf tissue and results in a yellow-green product of poor flavor. An ideal method is to lay the leafy shoots on slatted racks or frames covered with chicken wire. Place these in a warm, airy shed or airing cupboard. Alternatively, tie the herbs into small bunches and hang them up. A temperature between 80°–100°F (26.5° – 38°C) must be aimed at. If a room or shed is chosen, it is advisable to run an electric fan to

Herbs are easily dried by tying the cut stems into small bunches, using five to 10 stems depending on their bushiness (right). Hang these in a warm, airy place. A quicker method is to pick off the leaves and spread them on slatted shelves or frames of wire (below).

provide a current of air through, or over, the herbs. A third method is to use a cool oven, ideally one heated by solid fuel, leaving the oven door ajar.

Drying time varies with each herb and the method used. As soon as the leaves rattle when shaken or make a noise when touched, they are ready. Flowers should feel papery but should not break into dusty fragments when pressed between thumb and forefinger. Seeds must be dry and rattle when shaken, some falling off, while roots must be dry right through and snap readily.

STORING Dried herbs must be stored correctly or all the care in the drying process will be largely wasted. Once the drying is complete, allow the herbs to cool to room temperature and then immediately seal them in containers. Glass jars with airtight lids are still the best for this purpose, though quality plastic containers are almost as good. The containers must either be opaque or be stored in the dark, because exposure to light will bleach and spoil the herbs. Once containerized and sealed, keep the herbs in an even temperature. A larder or other place away from the steam of a kitchen is best. If it is necessary to have them in the kitchen, small containers, the contents of which can be used up quickly before deterioration takes place, are best. These can easily be filled from a main store. The same storage conditions should be provided for ripe seeds and dried fruits.

FREEZING Although deep freezing as a method of preserving herbs is comparatively recent, enough is now known to show its limitations. Deep freezing tends to lessen the flavor, especially of those herbs which rely upon a volatile oil, and, when thawed out, leafy kinds are limp.

Frozen herbs are best used within six months, while those dried properly can last two years. On the other hand, many of the commonest sorts for use in cooking, such as chives, mint, basil, parsley and tarragon, all freeze successfully and are ideal for soups and casseroles. Blanching is unnecessary and seriously reduces the oil content. The easiest way to freeze herbs is to make up small bunches, either of one type or in prepared *bouquets garnis*; then place them in small plastic bags and freeze immediately. An alternative method is to chop the herbs finely and pack, with a little water, into ice-cube trays. When frozen solid, it is best to wrap the cubes individually in foil. Chives, mint and parsley are particularly successful when treated this way and the cubes can be dropped straight into a casserole without thawing first.

Collecting seeds

Seed herbs are dried in the same way as leafy varieties. Removing the fully ripe seeds can be tricky, however, and it is best to put the seed heads in paper bags first to prevent spillage. When the seeds can be shaken or rubbed from their stems, remove and clean them, then store in opaque, sealable containers.

Allium cepa
EVER-READY ONION

This herb and the similar welsh onion (*A. fistulosum*) are clump-forming onions, grown mainly for their leaves. Both are like robust chives but the Welsh onion has leaves cylindrical in cross section and it flowers readily, whereas ever-ready onion has somewhat flattened leaves and rarely flowers. Both types can be lifted and eaten as a substitute for spring onions.

Propagation *Division in spring is the usual means of increase.*
Soil *Moderately fertile soil, moist but well drained, is the ideal. In dry, poor soils growth will be slow and the vegetable tough.*
Position *A sunny location is best, but half-day shade is tolerated.*
Cultivation *Young plants or divisions are best set out in their permanent sites in spring. The clumps should be divided regularly, at least every other year, to maintain a supply of plants. Apply fertilizer annually in spring.*

When harvesting ever-ready onions, lift whole clumps (right) and separate into individual shoots or bulbs

To increase your supply of small clumps for harvesting, divide (far right) and replant annually during the spring.

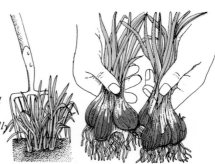

Allium sativum
GARLIC

This bulbous perennial is now grown throughout the world and is one of the most popular members of the onion family for flavoring. The white-skinned bulb is composed of several smaller bulbs or cloves and bears slender, flattened leaves to 1 ft (30 cm) long. Scientists have now confirmed that the substance allicin, which garlic contains, has anti-bacterial properties.

Propagation *Planting cloves is the easiest means of increase.*
Soil *Well-drained, ideally humus-rich soil is best.*
Position *A sunny site is essential. In cool summer areas, a sheltered, warm place is advisable.*
Cultivation *Plant individual cloves in spring or, in mild winter areas, in fall. Weed regularly and water during dry spells. When the foliage yellows in fall, lift the plants, tie in bundles and hang up to dry.*

To propagate garlic, take a whole bulb and carefully separate the cloves by pushing each one outwards.

Set out the cloves in prepared soil in spring, placing each one upright, 9 in (23 cm) apart and with 2 in (5 cm) of soil above the tip when the hole is filled.

Fully grown plants will be at least 1 ft (30 cm) tall, with flattened leaves. When the plants turn yellow, lift and dry off rapidly.

Allium Shoenoprasum
CHIVES

Common chives are the best known of clump-forming perennial onions grown primarily for their leaves. This species grows wild throughout the northern temperate zone. It is densely clump-forming, with slender, tubular leaves and globular clusters of rose or red-purple flowers on 1 ft (30 cm) tall stems in summer. It is a true herbaceous perennial, dying back to ground level in fall.

Propagation *Divide clumps or sow seeds in spring.*
Soil *A moderately fertile, moist but well-drained soil is the ideal, though reasonable results can be expected on poorer but not dry land.*
Position *A sunny site is best, though partial shade is acceptable.*
Cultivation *Set out in their permanent positions young plants from seeds in fall or divisions in spring. To maintain a vigorous supply of fresh leaves, several plants should be grown and cut in sequence. Liquid feed at monthly intervals.*

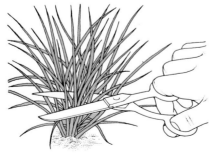

It is best to grow a batch of chive plants at any one time. Cut the leaves from each plant in turn, severing about 2 in (5 cm) above the ground. If six to ten plants are grown, by the time the last one has been harvested the first will be ready again.

Allium tuberosum
CHINESE CHIVES

Chinese chives are widely grown in the Orient, less commonly in the west. Clump-forming plants 1–1½ ft (30–45 cm) tall, Chinese chives have slim leaves which are solid in cross section (those of common chives are hollow). The white flowers are starry in appearance, carried in dense, rounded clusters in late summer and, unlike the majority of onion flowers, are fragrant, with the scent of heliotrope. These herbs are used in a variety of food dishes, both cooked and raw, where the flavor of onions is needed. The flavor is much stronger than that of ordinary chives and more nearly resembles garlic.

Propagation *Division in spring is the usual means of increase, although seed can be sown.*

Soil *A moist but not dry, moderately fertile soil is the ideal. Poorer soils must be dressed with organic matter.*

Position *A sunny site is best, though some morning or afternoon sun is tolerated, especially in hot summer areas.*

Cultivation *Set out young plants from seeds or divisions in their permanent sites in early fall or spring. Give plants that are being regularly cropped for use dressings of liquid fertilizer at monthly intervals from early summer to the end of fall.*

Aloysia triphylla
LEMON VERBENA

The botanical name of this deciduous shrub is controversial, some botanists favoring *Lippia citriodora*. In mild climates it can attain large shrub size, but in colder areas it is cut back to near ground level almost annually by frost. In severe winter areas it must be overwintered in a container under cover. The willow-like, bright green leaves are intensely lemon-fragrant.

Propagation *Cuttings are the primary means of increase. Softwood cuttings can be taken in spring or summer, hardwood cuttings in fall or early spring.*
Soil *A well-drained soil of moderate fertility is best.*
Position *A sunny location is essential.*
Cultivation *Set young plants out in their permanent sites once the weather warms up in spring. Alternatively, grow plants as specimens in tubs in cool areas. Except in the milder areas, those outside will need winter protection.*

Lemon verbena makes an attractive tub plant (right) for a patio in cold winter areas. When young, pinch out the stem tips regularly to promote an abundance of basal stems.

Tub specimens should be top-dressed annually (above). When the fresh soil is in position, firm it with the fists and water well.

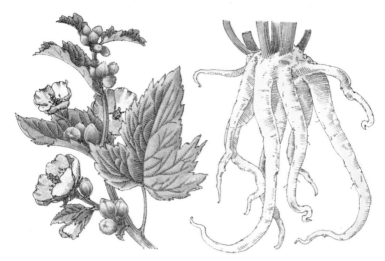

Althaea officinalis
MARSH MALLOW

In the wild, the marsh mallow inhabits the coastal marshes of Europe, north Africa and western Asia. It is naturalized in the United States. A clump-forming perennial to 6 ft (1.8 m) or more in height, it has gray, downy, lobed leaves to 3 in (7.5 cm) wide. Typically mallow-like, 1½ in (4 cm) wide pink flowers open in leafy spikes in late summer. The roots yield a mucilage used in confectionary and medicines. A tea can also be made with the dried roots to alleviate coughs and induce sleep. The lightly boiled leaves can be fried with sliced onions and served with bacon.

Propagation *Seed is the usual means of increase. Sow thinly in nursery rows in the spring, then thin the resulting seedlings to 1 ft (30 cm) apart. Alternatively, divide the plants in late winter or spring.*
Soil *Moist soil is required, ideally of moderate to good fertility. Poorer soil is best enriched with organic matter.*
Position *A sunny location is necessary to rear sturdy, leafy plants.*
Cultivation *Set out young plants in their permanent sites in early fall or spring. Water during dry spells, especially on the more porous soils. A mulch of organic matter each spring is beneficial.*

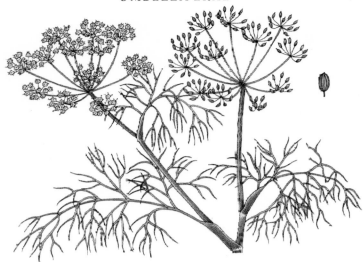

Anethum graveolens
DILL

Dill is an annual or biennial plant from eastern Europe and western Asia and was cultivated by the Greeks and Romans. It grows 2–3 ft (60–90 cm) tall, has leaves cut into thread-like segments and flattened heads of tiny yellow flowers. The spicily, anise-flavored leaves can be added to soups, stews and fish sauces.

Propagation *Seed is the only means of increase. In mild winter areas it can be sown in late summer, when large plants will result the following year. Elsewhere, sow in spring.*

Soil *Well-drained, fertile soil is required.*

Position *A sunny position is essential.*

Cultivation *Thin seedlings with care and space them about 10 in (25 cm) apart. They must be watered during dry spells and regularly weeded. When the plant has flowered and seeds start to brown, the stems of seed-heads should be cut and hung in a warm, airy place to complete drying.*

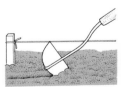
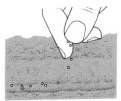

Seeds kept from a previous crop (left) can be used for propagation. Prepare the ground and make shallow drills (above).

Sow the seeds as thinly as possible (above) to reduce the need for thinning later. Then cover with a layer of fine soil.

Angelica Archangelica
ANGELICA

Sometimes known as *Archangelica officinalis*, angelica is a biennial or short lived perennial of imposing appearance if allowed to flower. It will attain 6–8 ft (1.8–2.4 m) in height. This herb is better known in its candied state as a decoration for cakes. For this purpose the leaf stalks and stems are gathered once the basal foliage has fully expanded.

Propagation *Seed is the best method of propagation, sown when ripe in late summer or fall, or in the following spring in nursery rows or on site.*
Soil *A moist, fertile soil is the ideal. Enrich poor soils with organic matter.*
Position *Light shade is best in warm summer areas. Full sun is tolerated, provided the soil is moist.*
Cultivation *Set out young plants raised in nursery rows in their permanent sites when they have about three true leaves. If sown on site, thin the seedlings at the seedleaf stage and keep them weeded and watered.*

For candying, the leaf stalks are used just as they approach full size. The bulky flowering stems can also be used when young, but they take a long time to candy and are usually less satisfactory.

Anthriscus Cerefolium
CHERVIL

Chervil is technically a biennial but, as leaves only are used, it is treated as an annual. The finely dissected leaves rival ferns in elegance. If allowed to mature, flowering stems 16–24 in (40–60 cm) tall develop, topped by flattened heads of tiny white flowers. Known also as salad chervil, this is a herb that deserves to be used more often. Its young leaves have a light flavor of anise combined with parsley and make a welcome salad garnish. Chopped leaves can be added to white sauce to accompany fish.

Propagation *Seed is the only means of increase. Sow thinly on site in spring, and indoors in late summer for a supply of leaves throughout the year.*
Soil *Any ordinary soil is suitable but preferably one that does not dry out rapidly and is of moderate fertility.*
Position *A sunny position is best in cool summer areas; partial shade is best in hot areas. Hot, very humid conditions are not appreciated.*
Cultivation *Seedlings must be regularly weeded with great care, and watered in dry areas. It is best to pinch out flowering stems when young.*

As only the leaves of chervil are used, everything should be done to foster their production. As soon as flowering stems are recognized low down in the center of the plant, pinch them out (right) and apply a liquid feed.

Armoracia rusticana
HORSERADISH

Horseradish is a vigorous, deep-rooted perennial with handsome, oblong, wavy leaves 1–2 ft (30–60 cm) in length. Spikes of small white flowers appear in early summer. The grated fresh roots of this herb have long been used to make a condiment sauce to accompany meat, especially beef. Its medicinal 'cure-all' properties are now little supported.

Propagation *Root cuttings (sets) about 9 in (23 cm) long are the usual means of increase.*

Soil *Moisture retaining but well-drained, fertile soil of good depth is ideal, though some sort of crop can be expected on poorer land.*

Position *A sunny location is best but partial shade is tolerated.*

Cultivation *Plant root cuttings 15–18 in (38–40 cm) apart in rows in spring. Water in dry spells and weed regularly. The crop is ready to lift in late fall. In severe winter areas, the roots should be lifted and stored in a cellar or similar frost-free place.*

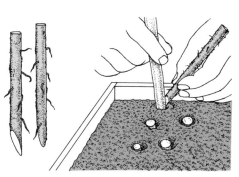

Root cuttings are the means by which horseradish plants are raised. Select roots the thickness of a pencil and cut them into 9 in (23 cm) lengths, severing the tops horizontally and the bases obliquely. Plant vertically, then cover with 2 in (5 cm) of soil.

Artemisia Abrotanum
SOUTHERNWOOD

Also known as old-man and lad's love, this herb has long been a favorite garden plant. It is now grown for its ornamental appearance and sweetly aromatic smell but it was once used as a tonic. It is a deciduous shrub to 3 ft (90 cm) or more tall, but it can be kept smaller by clipping. The finely-cut, gray-green leaves are 1–2½ in (2.5–6.5 cm) long.

Propagation *Take semi-hardwood cuttings in late summer but protect them in a coldframe during the winter in cold areas. In the milder winter areas, hardwood cuttings can be inserted on site in fall.*
Soil *A free-draining soil is the ideal. A moderately fertile soil is preferred but quite poor, chalky or sandy soil is acceptable.*
Position *A sunny location is best but half-day shade is tolerated.*
Cultivation *Young plants should be set out in their permanent sites in spring or fall. A light clipping in spring will maintain a compact habit.*

Southernwood must be clipped annually to keep it neat and bushy, but it stands more frequent clipping very well and then makes an attractive dwarf hedge for a herb garden.

Artemisia Dracunculus
TARRAGON

A perennial plant 2–3 ft (60–90 cm) tall, tarragon has a wide-spreading rootstock that can be invasive in rich soils. There are two types of tarragon, French and Russian. The latter is the hardier but the French variety has the better flavor. Both have lance-shaped leaves, but those of the Russian kind are a paler green and rougher to the touch than French tarragon. This plant is best known as the flavoring ingredient of tarragon vinegar.

Propagation *Division of the rootstock at planting time is the easiest means of increase. Alternatively, leafy cuttings root readily in summer.*
Soil *A well-drained soil is best, ideally of moderate fertility only. The best growth is made in a slightly alkaline soil.*
Position *A location in sun is best but partial shade is tolerated.*
Cultivation *Young plants should be set out in their permanent positions in spring, or fall in mild winter areas. In cold winter areas Russian tarragon does better than the French variety.*

In cold winter areas, mound up tarragon plants in fall with coarse sand or dryish peat for protection. Remove again in spring when growth starts and fear of severe frost has passed.

Artemisia vulgaris
MUGWORT

T his wayside weed is seldom used now but in the past it was taken as a tonic and, before hops became popular, it was added to malt beers to clear them. It is widely distributed in the temperate zones of the northern hemisphere, readily populating waste places and in the United States regarded as a weed. Clump-forming, it grows 2–4 ft (60–120 cm) in height. It has deeply lobed leaves, the undersides of which are covered in a gray-white down.

Propagation *Division of established clumps in fall or spring is the easiest means of increase. Alternatively, seed can be sown in containers in spring.*
Soil *Any soil is suitable but handsome, leafy plants will result if it is of moderate fertility and reasonably well drained.*
Position *A sunny site is best but partial shade is tolerated.*
Cultivation *Young plants or divisions can be set out in their permanent sites in spring or fall. The stems of established plants should be cut back to near ground level in fall.*

Although by no means essential, it is worth cutting off the dead stems of mugwort in late fall for the sake of tidiness. Use pruning shears (secateurs) for this job as the stems are woody near the base.

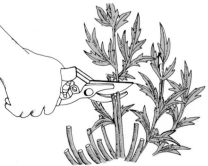

Borago officinalis
BORAGE

This annual herb is deservedly popular. Not only does it have culinary and medicinal uses, but it provides plenty of nectar and pollen for bees and pleases the eye with its sky-blue flowers. It grows 1–2 ft (30–60 cm) in height and has large, handsome, oval, bristly leaves and terminal clusters of flowers like nodding, five-pointed stars. The whole plant smells of cucumber when bruised.

Propagation *Seed is the most practical means of increase. This should be sown in spring, or fall in mild winter areas. Sow groups of two to three seeds where each plant is to mature, then thin to one seedling later.*
Soil *A well-drained but not dry, fertile soil is necessary to achieve a supply of tender young leaves. Enrich poorer soils with organic matter and fertilizer.*
Position *A place in full sun is best, though some shade is tolerated.*
Cultivation *Thin seedlings with care, give water during dry spells and weed regularly.*

The best plants of borage result from seed sown in the open ground. Rake the newly dug and firmed soil to a tilth.

Mark out shallow drills about 1 ft (3 cm) apart and ¼ in (6 mm) deep. Sow seeds in groups of three, 3 in (7.5 cm) apart.

When the seedlings have started to grow, thin out each group, leaving the most healthy seedlings to mature.

Calendula officinalis
POT MARIGOLD

In earlier times, the dried flowers of this highly ornamental annual were used to flavor soups and stews, while the fresh petals were and still are used to garnish salads. The juice of the plant was formerly considered to have healing properties for wounds. There are several handsome cultivars with double flowers, in shades of yellow and orange.

Propagation *Seed is the only means of increase. Sow thinly on site in spring or, in mild winter areas, in late summer or early fall. For an early display in cold winter areas, sow seed under cover in early spring at a medium temperature of 55–60°F (13–16°C).*

Soil *Almost any soil that is reasonably well drained and fertile is suitable.*

Position *A sunny location is best, though half-day shade is acceptable.*

Cultivation *Thin seedlings with care and weed regularly. Water in dry spells. Remove spent flower heads regularly to prolong the floral display.*

These days the petals of pot marigold flowers are the only part of the plant used for culinary purposes. To maintain a long succession of fresh flower heads, pick off all dead or dying blooms.

Capsicum annuum
PEPPERS

This herb must not be confused with the condiment black pepper, derived from ground and dried fruits of *Piper nigrum*. The capsicum is a tropical annual 1½–3 ft (45–90 cm) or more tall, with oval leaves and nodding, solitary white flowers. The fruits are used to flavor curries, sauces, pickles and salads.

Propagation *Seed is the only means of increase. Sow in mid-spring at a warm temperature of about 70°F (21°C).*
Soil *Well-drained but not dry soil, rich in organic matter, is the ideal.*
Position *A sunny and sheltered location is essential, especially in areas with cool summers.*
Cultivation *Young plants must not be set outside until all fear of frost has passed; place them 1–1½ ft (30–45 cm) apart. Pruning is not essential. Cane supports are advisable for tall cultivars. In cool summer areas, plants are best grown entirely under glass.*

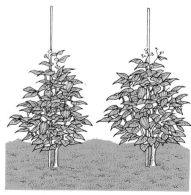

Although reasonably bushy and self-supporting, peppers are best tied to a strong cane. This is especially true for the large fruited, bell types, which can become top-heavy.

Carum Carvi
CARAWAY

This herb is grown as an annual or biennial, depending on the use to which it is to be put. It is a member of the carrot family. First year plants form rosettes of large leaves that are deeply dissected and have a ferny elegance. In the second year, stems to 2 ft (60 cm) or more arise, branching above and bearing flattened heads of tiny white flowers. The seeds that follow can be used to flavor rye bread, cakes, some cheeses and pickles. Caraway seeds can also be used in meat and fish dishes and in soups. Young leaves and stems, chopped finely, can be added to salads.

Propagation *Seed is the best means of propagation. Sow them on site or in nursery rows in early summer.*
Soil *A well-drained but not dry, fertile soil will give the best crop but growth is satisfactory in almost any ordinary soil.*
Position *A sunny, open place is necessary.*
Cultivation *Thin seedlings with care and keep regularly weeded. If young plants are to be moved from nursery rows, do so in early fall or spring. When seeds start to brown, cut the stems, bunch them and hang them heads downward in a warm, airy shed.*

Caraway is grown primarily for its aromatic seeds. When most of the seeds are brown, cut the stems (left).

Tie into small bunches and hang heads down in a warm, airy shed (right). As soon as the seeds are dry and start to fall, rub off and store in opaque jars.

Chamaemelum nobile
CHAMOMILE

The common name of this attractive herb is sometimes spelled camomile and botanically it is still often listed under *Anthemis nobilis*. Of spreading habit, this evergreen perennial attains 6–12 in (15–30 cm) in height but only when flowering in summer. The leaves are divided into thread-fine segments, which create a mossy effect. Plants can be used to create a small, fragrant lawn.

Propagation *The usual means of increase is to sow seed or divide plants in spring. Alternatively, cuttings can be taken in spring or late summer.*
Soil *Well-drained soil is essential but quite poor land is acceptable. Heavy soils should have coarse sand or grit worked into the top 6 in (15 cm) to improve drainage and aeration.*
Position *A place in full sun is best, though a little morning or afternoon sun will suffice.*
Cultivation *Young plants are best set out in their permanent sites in spring. If making a lawn, space plants about 5 in (13 cm) apart each way.*

The mossy, aromatic foliage of chamomile makes a pleasing small lawn around a garden seat. Once the plants are established, shear them at intervals in summer to prevent flowering stems from forming.

Chenopodium Bonus–Henricus
GOOD-KING-HENRY

Although often grown in the herb garden, this plant is really a vegetable. Sometimes called mercury or all good, it is a clump-forming perennial from Europe and western Asia. In Europe and North America it is sometimes seen on waste ground around farms and by roadsides in a semi-naturalized state. This undoubtedly indicates its former use as a food plant and it is still grown for its young, spring shoots, which should be taken when about 4–6 in (10–15 cm) tall, cooked and served with butter in the manner of asparagus. The summer leaves can be used as a spinach substitute. Fully mature leaves are triangular in outline and about 4 in (10 cm) long; if allowed to produce its insignificant flowers, the plant can reach 1½–2 ft (45–60 cm) in height.

Propagation *Division of established plants in early fall or spring, or sowing seeds on site in spring, are the main means of increase.*
Soil *To produce a worthwhile crop of young shoots, a humus-rich soil, moist but well drained, is required.*
Position *A sunny site is best, but some shade is tolerated.*
Cultivation *Apply a dressing of organic matter and high nitrogen fertilizer annually in spring. The second spring after planting, cutting can begin. Once all the main shoots have been harvested, cutting must cease.*

Chrysanthemum Balsamita
COSTMARY

Also known as mint geranium or alecost, this is a clump-forming perennial 3 ft (90 cm) or more in height. The oblong leaves are about 4 in (10 cm) long and both smell and taste of balsam, with a dash of mint. The erect, branched stems terminate in clusters of small flower heads that may look like either daisies or tansy buttons, depending on whether or not the white ray florets (petals) are present. The leaves are used to flavor soups, stews and ales and, like mint, can be added to iced tea and punches.

Propagation *Division of mature plants is the usual means of increase. Alternatively, sow seed in nursery rows.*
Soil *Ordinary, moderately fertile soil that does not readily dry out is the ideal. Poorer soils benefit from the addition of organic matter.*
Position *A sunny site is best though partial shade is tolerated, especially in warm summer areas.*
Cultivation *Young plants from seeds or divisions should be set out in their permanent sites in fall or spring. They must be watered during dry spells, especially on the more sharply draining soils.*

Dry the large basal leaves of costmary as soon as they reach full size. Sever the stalks, then place the leaves on wire frames or slatted shelves in a warm, dry place out of direct sun. Alternatively, put them in a cool oven until dry.

Chrysanthemum Parthenium
FEVERFEW

Feverfew is a short-lived perennial with deeply lobed leaves and large clusters of small white daisies. About 2 ft (60 cm) is the average height but dwarf forms are sold by seedsmen under the synonym *Matricaria capensis*. There are yellow-leaved and double flowered cultivars. As its name indicates, this herb was used to combat fevers. It was also considered beneficial for coughs and as a tonic. The leaves can be used to flavor soups and stews.

Propagation *Seed is the usual means of increase. This can be sown in early spring at a medium temperature of 55–60°F (13–16°C) or on site in mid- to late spring.*
Soil *Almost any soil is suitable, providing it is reasonably well drained.*
Position *A sunny site produces the most compact and floriferous plants but growth is satisfactory in up to half-day shade.*
Cultivation *Young plants raised under cover should not be set outside until the likelihood of severe frost has passed. In harsh winter areas, plants grown as perennials will need protection.*

In cold winter areas feverfew is best grown as an annual. However, it is possible to overwinter plants outside by protecting them with burlap (hessian or sacking) or plastic sheeting screens. Surround the plant with stakes (left) and then erect the screen around them (right).

Cichorium Intybus
CHICORY

This biennial plant, also known as witloof, is most familiar as a salad vegetable. Dig up mature roots in early winter and cut off the leaves about ½ in (1 cm) above the crown. Pack the roots in boxes of soil or peat and keep in the dark at about 55°F (13°C). The bud-like shoots (chicons) make an excellent salad ingredient and the dried and ground roots are used as a coffee adulterant. Chicory produces stems 3–4 ft (90–120 cm) tall, bearing blue dandelion-like flowers if allowed to grow the second year.

Propagation *Seed is the only means of increase. Sow thinly in early summer.*
Soil *A moist but not wet, moderately rich soil is needed for the production of good roots. Poor soils must be enriched with organic matter.*
Position *A sunny site is best, though some half-day shade is tolerated.*
Cultivation *Seedlings must be thinned with care, kept watered during dry spells and regularly weeded. Thin the plants to 10 in (25 cm) apart.*

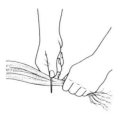

To produce chicons, dig up mature chicory roots, cut off the leaves ½ in (1 cm) above the crown and the root tip 8 in (20 cm) below.

Place the roots close together vertically in pots or boxes of peat or sandy soil.

Cover with another box or pot to exclude light and keep at about 55°F (13°C).

Coriandrum sativum
CORIANDER

Coriander is an annual to 1½ ft (45 cm) or more tall. The plants have both basal pinnate leaves, composed of pairs of oval leaflets, and finely dissected stem leaves. The tiny white, rose or lavender flowers are borne in small, flattened heads. The seeds of this herb of the carrot family are widely used to flavor confectionary, soups and alcoholic drinks. Young seeds have an unpleasant smell but when fully mature and after several months storage they take on a spicy orange fragrance.

Propagation *Seed is the only means of increase. This should be sown thinly in rows at least 1 ft (30 cm) apart in spring. In mild winter areas, seed can be sown in fall.*
Soil *A well-drained, ordinary soil is required. Rich, moist soils produce sappy plants and seeds, which lack flavor and aroma.*
Position *A sunny site is essential, warm and sheltered in cool summer areas.*
Cultivation *Seedlings must be thinned with care as soon as they are large enough to handle, allowing 3–4 in (7.5–10 cm) between the remaining plants. Weeding must be attended to regularly.*

Coriander resents root disturbance, so the seed must be sown where the plants are to mature. Rake the prepared soil to a good tilth, then mark out drills with a garden line or straight-edged board. Sow thinly and cover with no more than ½ in (1 cm) of soil.

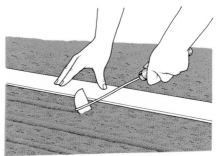

Cuminum Cyminum
CUMIN

Cumin is a slender, stalked annual and grows to about 10 in (25 cm) tall, with finely dissected blue-green leaves and clusters of small white and pink flowers. The seeds are an essential ingredient of curry powders and are used in mixed spices. They are also used to flavor bread, cakes, cheese, sausages and other sweet and savory dishes.

Propagation *Seed is the only means of increase. In warm areas, sow thinly in rows on site in spring. In cool summer areas, three to four seeds should be sown in 3 in (7.5 cm) pots in early to mid-spring at a warm temperature of about 60°F (16°C) and planted out later.*

Soil *Ordinary well-drained soil is suitable, preferably of moderate fertility.*

Position *A sunny site is essential.*

Cultivation *The seedlings must be thinned carefully to 3 in (7.5 cm) apart as soon as they are large enough to handle. Keep regularly weeded and watered in dry spells. In fall, cut the seeding stems and hang them to dry in a warm, airy place.*

Like coriander, cumin resents root disturbance and is best sown on site. In cool areas, however, a few seeds can be sown in 3 in (7.5 cm) containers.

Use a good quality seed-sowing mix. Cover the pots with glass or plastic sheeting and keep at about 60°F (16°C).

When the seedlings are large enough to handle, thin carefully to two or three seedlings per pot. Plant out together when the weather is suitable.

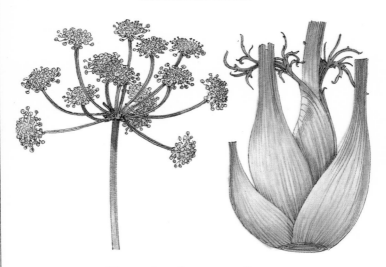

Foeniculum vulgare
FENNEL

Fennel is a clump-forming perennial to 6 ft (1.8 m) in height. The tall basal leaves, cut into thread-like, dark green filaments, make a most attractive, frothy mound. The erect, wind-proof stems branch above and bear flattened heads of tiny yellow flowers. Fennel was formerly used medicinally but is now grown for its leaves, which can be used to enhance fish sauces, soups and stews. *F.v.* 'azoricum' is the Florence or finnocchio fennel and has a flattened, bulb-like base which is eaten as a vegetable, either cooked or raw. Less commonly seen is *F.v. piperitum* (carosella). This is more like the common fennel in appearance but the leaves are shorter and stiff, composed of ½ in (1 cm) long, fleshy, rigid segments. It is grown for its young shoots, which are eaten as a vegetable.

Propagation *Seed is the usual means of increase, sown in spring on site or in nursery rows. Alternatively, divide mature plants in spring.*
Soil *A well-drained soil is essential, ideally of moderate fertility though poor, sandy or chalky soils are acceptable.*
Position *A sunny site gives the sturdiest plants but a little morning or afternoon shade is tolerated.*
Cultivation *Young plants can be set out in their permanent sites in spring or fall. If foliage only is required, cut out the flowering stems while still young.*

Galium odoratum
SWEET WOODRUFF

Classified by some botanists as *Asperula odorata*, woodruff is an herbaceous perennial forming wide colonies of erect, slender stems about 6 in (15 cm) tall. The whorls of slender, bright green leaves are like the spokes of a wheel. Small, tubular, pure white flowers open in terminal clusters in spring and early summer. The foliage contains coumarin, the substance that provides the scent of new mown grass. An infusion of the fresh foliage can be used as a tonic.

Propagation *Division at planting time is the easiest means. Alternatively, seed can be sown in spring.*
Soil *Ordinary soil is satisfactory but one well laced with organic matter is best.*
Position *A place in partial or dappled shade is ideal, though on moist soils in cool summer areas sweet woodruff will tolerate sun.*
Cultivation *Set out young plants in their permanent positions in spring or fall. They make good ground cover around trees and shrubs. Elsewhere they can be invasive and should be confined by slates or tiles, inserted around the site.*

Sweet woodruff is one of the few herbs which thrives in shade. It also forms pleasant soft green mats, not easily colonized by weeds. It is thus a good ground cover plant for growing beneath shrubs and trees. For this purpose, set out young plants 10–12 in (25–30 cm) apart each way and keep hand weeded until they meet.

Glycyrrhiza glabra
LICORICE

Also spelt liquorice, this herb, best known as a flavoring for candy, is a perennial plant which spreads sideways underground and can be invasive. The stems attain 3 ft (90 cm) in height and are clothed in leaves formed of up to 11 elliptic leaflets. Spikes of small bluish pea flowers open in summer and fall.

Propagation *Division of established plants in spring is the easiest means of increase. Alternatively, sow seeds in a frame or nursery row in spring. Then thin seedlings to 6 in (15 cm) apart.*
Soil *Moist but not wet soil produces the best rhizomes, from which the flavoring is extracted.*
Position *A sunny place is best but partial shade is tolerated.*
Cultivation *Young plants can be set out in their permanent sites in early fall or spring. It is best to confine the creeping rhizomes with tiles or slates, sunk vertically around the site.*

In some soils and situations, licorice can be invasive and it is always wise to confine the roots when planting this herb. Vertical slates or tiles sunk into the ground to enclose the plant are effective or each plant can be placed in an old, bottomless bucket sunk into the ground.

Helichrysum angustifolium
EVERLASTING

Like lavender cotton, this plant is best known for its ornamental foliage. It has culinary uses, however, the leaves imparting a curry flavor to soups and stews and to stuffings. An evergreen shrub up to 2 ft (60 cm) in height and spread, its very narrow leaves are silvery-gray and the tiny yellow everlasting flower heads are carried in dense clusters. Visitors to its southern European homeland will see the curry plant in great colonies, sometimes covering rocky hillsides near the sea with its silvery foliage. Combined with other Mediterranean shrubs such as *Cistus* (rock rose), *Genista* (broom) and lavender, it makes excellent garden planting for a dry, sunny site.

Propagation *Cuttings taken either in late summer or in spring provide an easy means of increase.*
Soil *Well-drained soil is essential but even dry, sandy or chalky sites are acceptable. Rich, moist soil promotes lush, uncharacteristic growth.*
Position *A sunny position is essential in cool summer areas. Hot sites are ideal, provided they are not also humid.*
Cultivation *Young plants are best set out in their permanent sites in spring. If a purely foliage effect is required, the flower stems should be pinched out when young. Either way, the plants are best trimmed or sheared over after flowering.*

Humulus Lupulus
HOPS

This is a perennial climber to 20 ft (6 m) which dies back each fall to a fleshy rootstock. The twining stems bear pairs of maple-like, three- to five-lobed leaves. Male and female flowers are borne on separate plants. Commercial hops are the mature female seed clusters, surrounded by leafy scales. Male flowers are carried in plumy clusters. Best known as the flavoring and preservative of beer, hops were formerly used medicinally as a tonic and as a soporific.

Propagation *Seed is the usual means of increase, sown in a frame in spring.*
Soil *A moist, fertile soil is the ideal, though acceptable results can be expected in drier or poorer soils.*
Position *A sunny site is required or one where the upper part of the plant is in sun, the base in shade.*
Cultivation *Set out young plants in their permanent sites in spring or fall. Provide a support of strings, netting or trellis and the plants will make a good summer screen. Apply organic matter in spring, at least every other year.*

Hop plants are fast, strong-growing climbers with firmly twining stems. A useful support can be made with an 8–10 ft (2.4–3 m) framework and poles (above) for the stems to twine around. Stems may need some encouragement to twine around the poles at first (left).

Hyssopus officinalis
HYSSOP

This herb is a perennial sub-shrub with a woody, shrub-like base. The pungently aromatic leaves are very narrow but abundantly borne. In summer, 1–1½ ft (30–45 cm) tall spikes of small purple-blue flowers open. Pink and white forms are available. Valued as both an ornamental and herb plant, hyssop must be used sparingly when flavoring food.

Propagation *Sow seed on site or divide mature plants in spring. Cuttings root readily in summer.*

Soil *Well-drained soil is essential but even poor, dryish, sandy or alkaline soil is tolerated.*

Position *For compact, densely leafed plants a sunny site is best, though some morning or afternoon shade is acceptable.*

Cultivation *Young plants can be set out in their permanent sites in spring or early fall. To keep the plants low and bushy, shear them over each spring or after flowering in mild winter areas.*

Although shrub-like, hyssop is best grown like a herbaceous perennial. Cut back plants with shears each spring to within 2 in (5 cm) of ground level as young growth starts.

Inula Helenium
ELECAMPANE

The root of this plant was formerly much used in a decoction to relieve coughs, asthma and bronchitis. Nowadays it is more likely to grace the flower garden with its imposing presence. It is a robust, clump-forming perennial to 6 ft (1.8 m) or more, with huge, oval, long-stalked basal leaves. The erect, wind-proof stems branch above, each side stem terminating in one or more bright yellow daisy-like flowers, about 3 in (7.5 cm) wide in late summer.

Propagation *Division of established plants in fall or spring is the easiest method. Seed can be sown in nursery rows in spring.*
Soil *The best results are achieved if the soil is moderately fertile and moist but not wet.*
Position *A sunny site is best though up to half-day shade is tolerated. If the soil is not particularly moist, some shade during the middle part of the day is beneficial.*
Cultivation *Young plants from seed or division can be set out in their permanent sites during fall or spring. Watering is advisable during dry spells.*

This massive, hardy perennial looks out of place in a herb garden unless used as the centerpiece of a collection. It is often better at the back of a border of mixed perennials or planted among shrubs.

Laurus nobilis

BAY

Also known as sweet bay, this flavoring herb is an attractive evergreen tree from the Mediterranean region. In mild winter areas it can exceed 30 ft (10 m) and exceptional specimens are twice this. Bay responds well to root restriction and regular clipping or pruning, however, and then makes a good tub or pot plant.

Propagation *Stem cuttings about 4 in (10 cm) long root readily in late summer or early fall. Seeds can be sown when ripe. Both must be kept above freezing point during their first winter.*
Soil *Ordinary garden soil that is well drained but not dry is satisfactory. Poor soils should be enriched with organic matter. If grown in a container, a soil-based potting mix is best.*
Position *Sun or partial shade is equally acceptable, but shelter from cold winds is needed.*
Cultivation *Where temperatures drop to 5°F (−15°C), winter protection must be given. Ideally, the plants should be grown in containers and overwintered under cover with a minimum temperature around freezing point.*

Bay trees respond well to root restriction and regular clipping or pruning. They are ideal, therefore, as container plants. A plant can be allowed to grow naturally; it can be clipped into a formal shape such as a pyramid or trained as a standard. Clip or prune shaped plants during the summer.

Unclipped   Pyramid   Standard

Levisticum officinale
LOVAGE

Lovage is a clump-forming perennial from Europe and western Asia, with robust, erect stems to 8 ft (2.4 m) in height. The leaves are divided into oval, coarsely-toothed leaflets and are rather like celery. The tiny, greenish-yellow flowers are borne in flattened heads in summer. The stems can be candied like those of angelica and the leaves impart a yeasty-celery flavor to soups, stews and cheeses.

Propagation *Divide plants or sow seed in spring.*
Soil *Moist but not wet, fertile soil gives the best results.*
Position *A sunny site is best but partial shade is tolerated, especially in hot summer areas.*
Cultivation *Set out young plants in their permanent sites in early fall or spring and water during dry spells. Wrapping the clumps of young leaves with paper or straw to exclude light, or drawing the soil up around them, will produce blanched stalks that are more palatable and better for candying than green ones.*

Like celery, the leaf stalks of lovage are most palatable if they are blanched. A quick method is to tie the leaves loosely together, then pack straw thickly around them so that only the leafy tops protrude. Blanching takes two to three weeks.

Marrubium vulgare
HOREHOUND

Also listed as common or white horehound, this relative of the dead nettles is an evergreen perennial, 1–2 ft (30–60 cm) in height. Clump-forming in habit, it has a gray appearance due to a covering of fine white hairs. The rounded leaves have a finely corrugated texture. From summer to fall, whorled spikes of small, tubular, off-white flowers appear. Before the use of hops, it was one of several herbs used to flavor beer.

Propagation *Sow seed thinly on site in spring or earlier under cover. Another method is to divide plants in spring.*
Soil *Any ordinary, well-drained soil is suitable, and even poor, alkaline or sandy soils are adequate.*
Position *A sunny site is essential to develop this herb's medicinal properties.*
Cultivation *Set out young plants in their permanent sites in early fall or spring. In areas of severe winters, some protection may be necessary. Cut back old stems of the previous year in spring.*

Horehound is a somewhat woody-based perennial and becomes untidy if not trimmed. In early spring, cut back the tops to about 3 in (7.5 cm) above ground level to keep the plants neat and bushy.

Melissa officinalis
BALM

Also aptly known as lemon balm, this clump-forming perennial has long had a place in herb gardens. The leaves, when bruised, are strongly fragrant of lemons and can be used fresh chopped in salads and to flavor cider and wine punches. Fresh and dried, they can be mixed with other herbs and used for stuffings and to make a tea. Balm grows 2–3 ft (60–90 cm) in height, with bright green, heart-shaped, crinkly leaves. In late summer, small, white, tubular, two-lipped flowers open in the upper leaf axils. In moist, fertile soils, lemon balm soon forms very wide clumps and can produce self-sown seedlings. In such soil conditions, contain the plants by inserting slates or tiles vertically in the ground to form a root-proof compartment. Seeding stems should be removed before the seeds are ripe. *M.o.* 'Aurea' has attractive yellow variegated leaves.

Propagation *Division in spring or fall is the easiest means of increasing balm. Alternatively, sow seed on site or in nursery rows.*
Soil *Almost any ordinary soil is suitable, but one that is fertile, well drained but not dry is the ideal.*
Position *Sunny and lightly shaded sites are suitable. In hot summer areas partial shade is best.*
Cultivation *Set out divisions or young plants from seed in spring or fall. Water during dry spells. Mature plants are best divided and replanted every three years or thereabouts.*

Mentha aquatica
WATER MINT

Although a parent of several very useful garden mints, the water mint is no longer as widely grown as it was. A native of Europe, Asia and North America, it grows 1–2 ft (30–60 cm) or more tall with toothed, oval leaves 1¼–3½ in (3–9 cm) in length, which are often purple-flushed. The whole plant smells strongly of peppermint. In summer, tiny lilac flowers open in whorled spikes. *M.a.* 'Crispa' is a curiosity, having crimped, cut leaves. It is sometimes grown for its ornamental appearance alone.

Propagation *Division in spring is the easiest and usual means of increase; make sure each division has about 6 in (15 cm) of rhizome attached.*
Soil *Moist soil of moderate fertility is required.*
Position *A place in sun is best but partial shade is tolerated.*
Cultivation *Set divisions in their permanent sites in spring or in fall in areas with mild climates. The root system is invasive and must be confined with vertical slates or tiles or planted in a sunken, bottomless pail.*

All mints are highly invasive plants, especially in moist, fertile soils. For this reason, the creeping, underground stems must be confined. An old, bottomless pail sunk in the soil is ideal for this purpose.

Mentha × gentilis
RED OR SCOTCH MINT

Red or scotch mint is a hybrid between spearmint (*M. spicata*) and field mint (*M. arvensis*). Of vigorous growth, it reaches to 2 ft (60 cm) or more in height, with lance-shaped to elliptic leaves 1½–2¾ in (4–7 cm) long. The plant smells of spearmint and is often red tinted. Tiny lilac flowers open in dense whorls in the upper leaf axils during the late summer.

Propagation *Division in fall or early spring is the easiest means of increase; pieces of healthy rhizome about 6 in (15 cm) in length should be chosen. Leafy stem cuttings root readily in early summer.*
Soil *Almost any soil that is not too dry will serve.*
Position *Sun or partial shade are equally suitable.*
Cultivation *Young plants from cuttings or division of the rhizomes can be set out in their permanent sites in fall or spring. Red mint is invasive and should be confined with vertical slates or grown in an old, bottomless pail sunk into the soil.*

One way of confining the creeping rhizomes of mint is to use it as a centerpiece to a small herb garden, which has been designed with paving or brick sets cemented into position. Variegated red mint (M. × *gentilis 'Aureo-Variegata'), with its ornamental foliage is ideal for such a position.*

Mentha × piperita
PEPPERMINT

Curiously enough, the peppermint plant and the lemon or bergamot mint of commerce are both expressions of the same hybrid, a cross between the spearmint (*M. spicata*) and the water mint (*M. aquatica*). Lemon mint (*M. × p. citrata*) is also known in Europe as Eau-de-Cologne mint and this name aptly describes the scent of its bruised leaves. In appearance it is most similar to water mint, with stems to 2 ft (60 cm) tall and oval leaves. Peppermint grows taller and has narrower leaves. The form grown in the United States for its peppermint oil has deep purple stems and tinted leaves and is known as black peppermint. White peppermint (*M. × p. officinalis*) lacks the purple pigment and has narrower leaves. Although of hybrid origin, the pepper and lemon mints and their forms are extensively naturalized in Europe and the United States. Peppermint oil is used extensively in confectionary.

Propagation *Division in fall or spring is the easiest method. Alternatively, cuttings root easily in summer.*
Soil *A moist soil is the ideal, but good growth is made on all ordinary soils.*
Position *Sunny or shady sites are equally suitable.*
Cultivation *Divisions of rhizomes or young plants from cuttings should be set out in their permanent sites in spring or fall. Mint plants are invasive and the rhizomes should be confined with vertical slates or grown in an old bottomless pail sunk into the ground. Rhizomes lifted and containerized in the fall can be brought indoors in winter for an early supply of leaves.*

Mentha Pulegium
PENNYROYAL

Botanically, pennyroyal is a mint. It has a mat-like habit, with erect stems to about 1 ft (30 cm). It can be used to make a small, fragrant lawn by itself or mixed with grasses. This herb stands mowing remarkably well.

Propagation *Division, in spring or fall, is the usual method of increase.*
Soil *A moist but not necessarily wet, moderately fertile soil is needed. It will also grow in a really wet position, such as the edge of a pond.*
Position *A sunny site is best, though a little shade is tolerated.*
Cultivation *Set out young plants in their permanent sites in early fall or spring. To make a lawn, plant them about 8–10 in (20–25 cm) apart each way. Water during dry spells, especially on soils that are not moist.*

In the wild, pennyroyal is often found among grasses and other plants by ponds and streams. This can be attractively copied in the garden to form a small, fragrant lawn. When cutting the lawn, set the lawn-mower blades high.

Mentha spicata
SPEARMINT

This is probably the most popular mint suitable for making sauce to accompany meat. It grows 2–3 ft (60–90 cm) in height with lance-shaped, sharply toothed leaves 2–3½ in (5–9 cm) long. Tiny white, pink or lilac flowers are borne in densely whorled spikes from late summer onward. Apart from its wide use in mint sauce, spearmint can be used to flavor vegetables such as peas and potatoes. Spearmint is also used as the flavoring in the green liqueur *creme de menthe*.

Horsemint (*M. longifolia*) is much like a gray or white downy spearmint. The form most frequently cultivated is densely white and downy, making a handsome foliage plant. However, the rhizomes must be kept in check since they spread rapidly.

Propagation *Division in early spring is the easiest means of increase; pieces of healthy rhizome about 6 in (15 cm) in length must be chosen. Leafy stem cuttings root readily in early summer.*
Soil *Almost any soil that is not too dry will serve.*
Position *Sun or partial shade are equally suitable.*
Cultivation *Young plants from cuttings or division of the rhizomes can be set out in their permanent sites in fall or spring. Spearmint, like all mints, is invasive and should be confined with vertical slates or grown in an old, bottomless pail sunk into the soil.*

Mentha suaveolens
APPLE MINT

Apple mint is a robust plant 3–4 ft (90–120 cm) high, with broadly oblong, white hairy leaves 1¼–1¾ in (3–4.5 cm) long. It is often confused with *M. × rotundifolia*, a hybrid form. Very similar but even more robust is *M. × villosa alopecuroides*. It, too, is sometimes confused with *M. suaveolens* but it has leaves more than 2 in (5 cm) long. Apple mint is highly flavored and, because of this, ideal for making mint sauce. However, the woolly appearance of its leaves tends to make it less popular for this purpose than its smooth-leaved relation, spearmint.

Propagation *Division in fall or spring is the easiest method; cuttings root easily in summer.*
Soil *A moist soil is the ideal, but growth is made on most soils.*
Position *Sunny or shaded sites are equally suitable.*
Cultivation *Division of roots (rhizomes) or young plants from cuttings should be set out in permanent sites in spring or fall. Mint plants are invasive and the rhizomes must be confined with vertical slates or grown in an old bottomless pail.*

One way to lessen attacks of mint rust, a common disorder of mints, is to raise young plants regularly from cuttings in summer. Take leafy shoots about 3–4 in (7.5–10 cm) long, ideally of sturdy side stems. Dip the stems in rooting powder and then plant around the edge of small pots of sandy soil. Keep the cuttings in humid conditions until they have rooted.

Menyanthes trifoliata
BOGBEAN

Also known as marsh trefoil, this decorative plant seems to have nothing in common with the gentian in spite of the family to which it belongs. Indeed, some botanists now put it in a family of its own, the *Menyanthaceae*. It is essentially a plant of wet habitats and looks best with its long horizontal stems (rhizomes) floating just beneath the water, the big trefoil leaves standing above. The intriguing flowers look as if they are cut out of toweling.

Propagation *Division is the usual means of increase but the long rhizomes can be cut into 4–6 in (10–15 cm) lengths and planted on site in spring.*
Soil *Permanently moist soil is essential, an ideal site being at the edge of a pond.*
Position *A place in full sun is best; some shade is tolerated, though flowering will be less prolific.*
Cultivation *Young plants can be set directly into their flowering sites at any time, but ideally in spring. Established plants are invasive and are best cut back or divided every three years.*

The most effective way to grow bogbean is to plant it in the moist soil at the edge of a pond. The rhizomes will spread out beneath the surface of the water, and the leaves will form a decorative covering.

Monarda fistulosa
BERGAMOT

The common name of this plant can be confusing to the novice. The bergamot oil of commerce comes from *Citrus aurantium Bergamia*, a variety of the Seville orange. In temperate countries, however, two members of the genus *Monarda* have acquired this name, both native to North America. In the United States wild bergamot is *M. fistulosa*, while in the United Kingdom *M. didyma* bears this name. The plants are similar, being clump-forming perennials to 3 ft (90 cm) tall and both are grown in flower beds and borders.

Propagation *Division in fall or spring is the easiest means of increase. Sow seed in spring, ideally under cover as the seedlings are very small and easily damaged in bad weather conditions.*
Soil *Most ordinary soils are suitable, though the best growth is achieved in those that are fertile and moist but well drained.*
Position *Sunny or partially sunny sites are equally acceptable, but if the soil is on the dry side partial shade is advisable.*
Cultivation *Set out divisions or plants raised from seed in their permanent sites in fall or spring. Water in dry spells.*

Myrrhis odorata
SWEET CICELY

This is a herbaceous perennial with handsome, finely divided, ferny, myrrh-scented leaves and erect stems to 3 ft (90 cm) or more, bearing flattened clusters of small white flowers, which should be left to produce seeds. It must not be confused with plants sharing the common name listed under the genus *Osmorhiza*, which have leaves cut into larger, lance-shaped oval leaflets.

Propagation *Seed is the usual means of increase. Sow on site, preferably as soon as the seeds ripen on the parent plant.*

Soil *A moisture retaining but not wet, fertile soil is the ideal and essential if the root is to be used.*

Position *Dappled shade is preferred, but it grows well in full sun providing the soil does not dry out rapidly.*

Cultivation *Thin seedlings with care and keep regularly watered and weeded. Transplant young plants in fall or spring 1½–2 ft (45–60 cm) apart.*

The seed of sweet Cicely is not long lived and must be sown as soon as ripe. To collect the seeds, cut off the seed heads, place in a bag and shake the seeds loose.

Select plump, black seeds as only the ripest, fully developed specimens will yield strong seedlings.

Sow the seeds in drills in a nursery row or where the plants are to grow. Space out at 2 in (5 cm) apart and cover with a ½ in (1 cm) layer of soil.

Myrtus communis
MYRTLE

The common myrtle has an ornamental appearance, which makes it an attractive centerpiece in a herb garden in mild areas. It is also a good container plant. An evergreen shrub 4–10 ft (1.2–3 m) in height, it has dark green, lance-shaped, aromatic leaves to 2 in (5 cm) long and white or pink tinged flowers in summer, each ¾ in (2 cm) wide with a crown of stamens.

Propagation *Take semi-hardwood cuttings, ideally with a heel attached, in late summer.*
Soil *A well-drained soil is essential, ideally of moderate fertility. For plants in containers, a loam-based potting mix is best but not essential.*
Position *A sunny place against a sheltered wall is essential in all but the mildest winter areas.*
Cultivation *Young plants must not be set in their permanent sites until fear of frost has passed. Where winters are severe, grow the plant in a container and overwinter in a protected position just above freezing point.*

In mild winter areas, common myrtle makes a choice evergreen centerpiece for a small, formal herb garden (left). Where winters are severe, grow myrtle in a tub that can stand outside during the summer, either on a patio or terrace.

Nasturtium officinale
WATERCRESS

Watercress has long been valued for its medicinal properties, being rich in vitamin C and mineral salts. Two closely allied species and their hybrids are involved, all members of the genus *Nasturtium* (*Rorippa*). All have fleshy stems to 1 ft (30 cm) or more long, bearing pinnate leaves, each with an extra large terminal leaflet. In *N. officinale* the leaves stay green; in *N. microphyllum* they flush bronze in fall.

Propagation *Cuttings, which should be set 6 in (15 cm) apart, are a common means of increase. Alternatively, sow seed in spring.*
Soil *Moderately rich soil is best, ideally in special beds fed with running water.*
Position *A location in sun or light shade is acceptable.*
Cultivation *The crop is grown commercially in running water from a cool stream or spring. In the garden, it can be grown in tanks or tubs with about 4 in (10 cm) of water over an equal depth of soil. Watercress of acceptable quality can also be grown in trenches, which must be flooded every few days or daily in hot weather.*

Few gardeners have a natural stream flowing through their garden to provide the ideal conditions for watercress. An alternative is to dig a trench at least 1 ft (30 cm) deep, work organic matter into the bottom and keep wet with frequent watering.

Nepetia Cataria
CATMINT

Catmint is a clump-forming perennial 2–3 ft (60–90 cm) tall with grayish hairy stems and leaves, and whorled spikes of small, purple-spotted white flowers. This plant holds a fascination for cats.

Propagation *Divide young shoots in late spring and keep in a cold frame; alternatively seed can be sown when ripe or in spring, preferably under cover but also in a nursery row outside.*

Soil *A well-drained and moderately fertile soil is required, though even fairly poor soils are tolerated.*

Position *A sunny, airy site is best, though a little morning or afternoon shade is tolerated.*

Cultivation *Young plants from division or seed can be set out in their permanent sites in fall or spring.*

Division is the easiest way to increase catmint. In spring, just as young growth can be seen, lift the plants and carefully pull the clump apart. If the clump is old, a knife may be needed to cut through the toughest parts. Replant the divisions immediately where they are to grow.

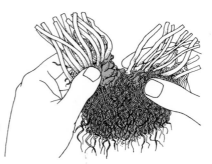

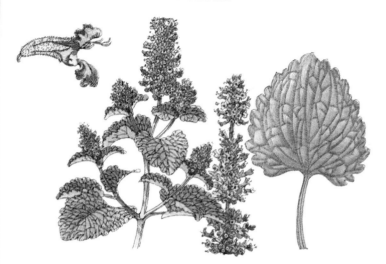

Ocimum Basilicum
BASIL

Several members of the genus *Ocimum* are known as basils, but only *O. Basilicum*, the common basil, is widely grown. It is used as a flavoring. Common basil grows 16–24 in (40–60 cm) tall and is bushy in habit, with oval to oblong toothed leaves and terminal spikes of small, white or purplish tubular flowers in late summer. *O.b.* 'Purpurascens' has coppery purple leaves; *O.b.* 'Minimum' is the bush basil, a small compact plant to 10 in (25 cm) tall.

Propagation *Seed is the only means of increase. Sow under cover in early to mid-spring at a warm temperature of about 60°F (16°C).*
Soil *A well-drained but not dry soil of moderate fertility is required. Poorer soils are best enriched with organic matter.*
Position *A sunny site is best, particularly in cool summer areas. Shelter from strong winds is also advisable.*
Cultivation *Basil is frost tender and young plants must not be set outside until fear of frost has passed and the weather warms up. Weeding must be thorough and watering is necessary during dry periods.*

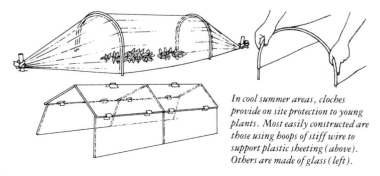

In cool summer areas, cloches provide on site protection to young plants. Most easily constructed are those using hoops of stiff wire to support plastic sheeting (above). Others are made of glass (left).

Origanum vulgare
OREGANO

Two members of this genus are given the name oregano. Best known is *O. vulgare*, which is also known as common marjoram. It is a clump-forming plant to 1½ ft (45 cm) or more, with a rather woody base and broadly oval leaves ¾–2 in (2–5 cm) long. Very small pink to white flowers mixed with tiny purplish bracts are carried in branched terminal clusters in summer. The other oregano, called winter marjoram, is *O. heracleoticum*. It resembles *O. vulgare* but has green floral bracts and a stronger aroma. Oregano has culinary and medicinal uses, and can be added to a pot-pourri. Confusingly, the Spanish thyme of Suganda (*Coleus amboinicus*) is also known as oregano. However, it is a very different plant, being a tender, soft-stemmed shrub to 3 ft (90 cm) with fleshy leaves and spikes of small, tubular, lavender-pink flowers. The 1–3 in (2.5–7.5 cm) long leaves are aromatic.

Propagation *Division or cuttings of young shoots in spring are the usual means of increase. Seed should be sown under cover in early spring at a medium temperature of 55–60°F (13–16°C).*

Soil *A well-drained soil is essential, ideally moderately fertile though poorer soil is acceptable.*

Position *A sunny location is best, although a little morning or afternoon shade is tolerated.*

Cultivation *Put young plants in their permanent sites in spring. In areas of prolonged frost, winter protection is needed or the plants must be grown in containers and kept under cover.*

Origanum Majorana
SWEET MARJORAM

Known also as knotted or garden marjoram, this is the most popular kind of marjoram for culinary and medicinal purposes. It is a woody-based perennial to 2 ft (60 cm) tall, with gray, hairy leaves to 1 in (2.5 cm) long. The small white or pinkish tubular flowers are borne in little spikelets, which in turn are gathered into terminal clusters. The whole plant is sweetly aromatic.

Propagation *Sow seed or take cuttings from overwintered plants in spring.*
Soil *A well-drained soil is essential, ideally of moderate fertility but not rich.*
Position *A sunny site is needed, especially in cool summer areas.*
Cultivation *Young plants must not be set outside until all fear of frost has passed. Only in mild winter areas will this herb behave as a perennial. In hot summer areas, it is advisable to shade seedlings from the midday sun.*

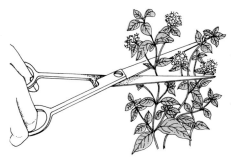

Sweet marjoram is the most popular kind of marjoram for cooking as it dries well and has a long storage life. For drying, cut the leafy stem just as the first flowers open and dry as rapidly as possible by hanging in an airy, shaded place.

Origanum Onites
POT MARJORAM

Three different herbs are known as marjoram, all members of the genus *Origanum*. Pot marjoram is a shrubby-based perennial reaching 1–2 ft (30–60 cm) tall with slender stems clad with small, oval, aromatic leaves. The tiny, tubular, white flowers are in small spikes, in turn grouped into larger, leafy clusters. The leaves have a bitter quality, reminiscent of thyme; when dried they are an important ingredient of *bouquet garnis* and are also used in stuffings and for seasoning.

Propagation *Division or cuttings, both undertaken in spring, are the easiest means of increase. Seed can be sown at the same time, ideally in a frame or greenhouse. It is slow to germinate.*
Soil *A well-drained soil is essential, ideally moderately fertile but not rich.*
Position *A sunny location is required, especially in cool summer areas.*
Cultivation *Set out young plants in their permanent sites in spring. In mild winter areas, marjoram is fully perennial. In cold winter areas it must be grown annually or overwintered either in a frame or indoors.*

Pot marjoram is a distinctive and pretty plant, well worth a place in a tub or window-box collection of herbs. A tub positioned on a terrace or patio makes an attractive feature and is useful if near the kitchen.

Pelargonium graveolens
SWEET GERANIUM

This is a soft shrub to 3 ft (90 cm) tall with deeply five-lobed leaves, boldly toothed and gray-green. The flowers, which vary from 1–1½ in (2.5–4 cm) across, are pink with purple veins and spots and are borne in stalked clusters in summer.

Propagation *Cuttings are the usual means of increase. Take them in late summer or in spring from overwintered plants.*
Soil *A well-drained soil is essential, ideally of moderate fertility. Rich soil produces over-large, soft, sappy growth.*
Position *Full sun is necessary for compact growth and strong fragrance.*
Cultivation *Young plants must not be set outside until all fear of frost has passed. They must be lifted and potted in fall and overwintered under cover. Alternatively, they can be grown permanently in containers kept outside in summer and inside in winter.*

The sweet geranium is easily raised from cuttings. Select strong but not over-thick or sappy stem tips.

Cut cleanly beneath a leaf so that the cutting is about 3–4 in (7.5–10 cm) long and remove the lower leaves.

Insert the cuttings around the edge of a pot of sandy soil. They root rapidly.

Petroselinum crispum
PARSLEY

Cultivated for at least 300 years, parsley remains one of the most popular of all herbs. It is primarily a biennial but can be grown as an annual. If the flowering stems are pinched out regularly, it will live from two to three years but young plants are best. It forms a tufted rosette of elaborately dissected, ferny leaves to about 6 in (15 cm) in height. The flowering stem attains 2 ft (60 cm) or more, with flat clusters of tiny greenish-yellow flowers.

Propagation *Seed is the only means of increase. Sow on site in spring, or earlier under cover at a medium temperature of 55°F (13°C) for an early crop.*
Soil *A well-drained but not dry, fertile soil is best.*
Position *A sunny location is preferred but partial shade is acceptable.*
Cultivation *Seedlings must be thinned with care, ideally in several stages until the final plants are spaced about 10 in (25 cm) apart. Weed regularly and water well during dry spells. For a winter crop where frosts are severe, plant in pots in fall and bring on under cover.*

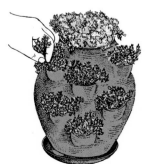

Parsley is easily grown, both in open ground and in a container. A particularly decorative method is to grow it in an earthenware parsley or strawberry pot, which can stand on a terrace, patio or veranda.

Petroselinum crispum 'tuberosum'
HAMBURG PARSLEY

Botanically, Hamburg parsley is a variety of the same species as common parsley. The *'tuberosum'* addition to its name refers to its swollen tap-root, which closely resembles a slim parsnip and is eaten as a vegetable. The foliage is taller and coarser than that of common parsley and more akin to the original wild plant. It can be used in exactly the same way as common parsley to flavor fish sauces and, when finely chopped, as a garnish. All parsley leaves are rich in vitamins A, C and D and contain iron, hence their value as a garnish.

Propagation *Seed is the only means of increase; sow thinly in spring just as the weather starts to warm up.*

Soil *A well-drained but moisture-retaining soil is essential for tender, fleshy roots to develop.*

Position *A sunny site is best, though a little shade is tolerated.*

Cultivation *Seedlings must be thinned progressively and carefully until a final spacing of 1 ft (30 cm) is achieved. Weeding must be regularly attended to and water given during dry spells.*

Pimpinella Anisum
ANISE

This native of Asia is widely naturalized elsewhere. It grows to 20 in (50 cm) or more tall, with coarsely pinnate basal leaves that become more deeply cut on the stem. The tiny, five-petalled flowers are white. It is an annual herb grown mainly for its seeds, which are used to flavor cakes, breads, candies and the liqueur anisette.

Propagation *Seed is the only means. Sow thinly in rows where the plants are to grow to maturity.*
Soil *Well-drained, fertile soil is required.*
Position *A site in full sun is essential, especially in cool summer areas, to be sure the seeds thoroughly ripen and dry for successful storing.*
Cultivation *Seedlings must be thinned with care to about 1 ft (30 cm) apart. Weed regularly and water, especially during dry spells. When the seeds turn pale brown, cut the stems, tie them in bundles and hang in a warm, airy place.*

As soon as about half of the seed crop has turned brown, cut the stems just above ground level and tie them in small bunches. Hang these in a warm, dry place until all the seeds are thoroughly ripe, then rub off the seeds and place in trays for a further week or so. Store in opaque, screw cap jars.

Polygonum Bistorta
BISTORT

Known in the United States as snakeweed, this plant is now more often grown for its floral display than its herbal uses. It is a widely clump-forming perennial with large, long-stalked, oblong basal leaves and poker-like spikes of pink flowers on 1½ ft (45 cm) tall stems in summer. *P.b.* 'Superbum' is larger and better for a flower border.

Propagation *Division of established plants in fall or spring is the easiest means of increase. Alternatively, sow seed in nursery rows when ripe or in spring.*
Soil *Moisture-retaining but not wet soil of moderate fertility is the ideal. Poorer soils are best enriched with organic matter.*
Position *Sun or partial shade are equally acceptable, though in drier soils partial shade is preferable.*
Cultivation *Divisions or young plants raised from seed can be set in their permanent positions in spring or fall. Water during dry spells.*

Whether bistort is to be used as an ornamental plant, as a herb or a vegetable, it pays to keep it mulched with organic matter. This stimulates fine large leaves and plenty of flower spikes. Well rotted manure is the best mulch, applied in spring. Peat together with a general fertilizer is a good substitute.

Poterium Sanguisorba
BURNET

The salad or garden burnet is one of the few members of the rose family to be grown in the herb garden; it can be added to salads. It is a clump-forming perennial, with densely-borne pinnate leaves and slender stems 16–24 in (40–60 cm) tall, which carry globular to cylindrical heads of tiny greenish, petalless flowers with red-purple stigmas.

Propagation *Seed may be sown on site in spring, but division at planting time is the easiest means of increase.*

Soil *A well-drained but not dry soil of moderate to high fertility is required. Poor land should be enriched with organic matter.*

Position *A sunny location is best but partial shade is tolerated, especially in warm summer areas.*

Cultivation *Young plants should be set out in their permanent sites in spring or early fall, spacing them 1 ft (30 cm) apart.*

To maintain a good supply of the useful and decorative leaves of burnet, prevent flowering stems from maturing. As soon as these are seen rising among the leaves, which may be from spring onward, pinch them out as low down as possible.

Primula veris
COWSLIP

The cowslip is now thought of mainly in terms of its beauty as a flowering plant. Formerly, an infusion of its flowers was believed to calm the nerves and induce sleep. Flowers are still sometimes used to make cowslip wine. Fresh flowers and leaves can be added to a salad, and the leaves, which are similar to those of watercress in flavor, are reputed to have tonic properties. The cowslip is a small, clump-forming perennial to 6 in (15 cm) or so tall with grayish-green, oblong leaves and one-sided clusters of fragrant, deep yellow flowers in spring. It has a wide range as a wild plant, being found throughout Europe and into Western Asia. It has several geographic variants (botanically subspecies), all of which have larger flowers than the western European form. Particularly attractive is *P.v. Columnae*, with richly colored flowers, and leaves which are hairy and white beneath. Largest flowered of all is *P.v. macrocalyx* from south-eastern Russia and the Crimea.

Propagation *Division of established plants after flowering or in early fall is the easiest means of increase. Sow seed when ripe or in spring.*
Soil *Well-drained but not dry, moderately fertile soil is the ideal, preferably alkaline in reaction.*
Position *A sunny site is required, though a little shade is tolerated, especially in warm summer areas. Cowslips do not usually thrive in hot, humid climates.*
Cultivation *Set out young plants in their permanent sites in spring or early fall. Water in warm, dry spells, spraying over-head at the same time.*

Rosmarinus officinalis
ROSEMARY

This evergreen shrub from the Mediterranean region has graced our gardens for centuries, its decorative appearance rivalling its culinary and medicinal value. It is a shrub of variable habit from mat-forming to erect, reaching 6½ ft (2 m) in height. Its spring- and summer-borne, violet-blue flowers attract bees. Regrettably, it is not hardy where winters are severe, cold or wet but it makes a good container plant for the summer patio.

Propagation *Take cuttings in late summer, or layer in spring.*
Soil *A well-drained soil is essential but poor, sandy or alkaline soils suffice.*
Position *A sunny location is best but in cool summer climates shelter from cold winds is necessary. It makes a good foundation planting at the foot of a house wall.*
Cultivation *Set out young plants in their permanent sites in spring when the worst of the frosts are over.*

Where temperatures do not drop below about 10°F (−12°C), rosemary can be grown as a foundation planting at the foot of a sheltered wall. The erect forms are particularly useful for this purpose. If a sheltered retaining dry wall is available, R. prostratus *will cover it decoratively.*

Rumex Acetosa
GARDEN SORREL

Garden sorrel is a clump-forming plant, which can attain 2–3 ft (60–90 cm) in height if allowed to flower. The dark green leaves, shaped like the head of a lance, are about 4 in (10 cm) long and thick-textured. Reddish, erect spikes of petalless flowers expand in summer but, unless seed is required, they are best removed when young. The leaves can be used as a spinach substitute or shredded raw and added to salads. Finely chopped, they make a garnish to egg dishes. Also known as sour dock, this sorrel has a very wide range in the wild, inhabiting grassland and open places in woodland throughout Europe and temperate Asia. It was introduced by early settlers to North America and is now found in meadows and by roadsides from Labrador to Alaska, south to Pennsylvania.

Propagation *Sow seed on site in spring to begin the crop. Thereafter, division in fall or spring is the easiest method.*
Soil *Well-drained but moisture retaining fertile soil is required for a good supply of tender leaves. Poor land should be enriched with organic matter.*
Position *A sunny location is the ideal, though partial shade is acceptable.*
Cultivation *Young plants from divisions should be set out 1 ft (30 cm) apart in rows in spring or early fall. Thin seedlings with care, keep them weeded regularly and water in dry spells.*

Rumex scutatus
FRENCH SORREL

French sorrel, though a close relation of garden sorrel, is very distinct in appearance, being a tufted to a clump-forming plant with prostrate to semi-reclining stems to 1½ ft (45 cm) or more in length. The leaves are gray-green and almost triangular in outline, but rarely more than 1½ in (4 cm) long. They are more acid than those of common sorrel and have a wider range of herbal uses. It is the best species for making sorrel sauce, to accompany poultry and fish dishes, and is the basis of the French *soupe des herbes*.

Propagation *Division in spring or fall is the easiest means of increase. Seed is also an easy method; sow thinly on site in spring.*
Soil *A moderately fertile soil is best but poorer soil is acceptable. It must be well drained but not dry.*
Position *A sunny site is the ideal but a little shade is tolerated.*
Cultivation *Keep seedlings and young plants weeded and watered during dry spells. They are best spaced 1 ft (30 cm) apart. Pinch out the flowering spikes while young.*

When preparing the site for a herb garden, it is important that perennial weeds are removed before planting. Fork the ground over at least one spit deep and hoe out all weed roots. Alternatively, when the weeds are in young growth use a systemic herbicide, which will allow planting very soon afterward.

Ruta graveolens
RUE

Of all the herbs grown in temperate climates, rue is the most bitter and pungently aromatic. In earlier times it was taken to restore failing eyesight. It was also taken as a tonic, the leaves being rich in iron and mineral salts. It is a sub-shrub to 2 ft (60 cm) or more tall, of bushy, rounded habit. The deeply dissected leaves are pale blue-green and very decorative. Uniquely formed, cup-petalled yellow flowers open in terminal clusters in summer. The cultivar *R.g.* 'Jackman's Blue' has the richest colored foliage.

Propagation *Plant seed under cover in spring or take cuttings in late summer.*
Soil *A freely-drained soil is essential for a long lived, compact plant. Sandy and poor soils are generally acceptable, though one of moderate fertility is best.*
Position *A location in full sun is ideal, though some morning or afternoon sun is tolerated.*
Cultivation *Set out young plants in their permanent sites in spring. In severe winter areas, it is best to keep a potted specimen under cover, where it will make a decorative plant.*

Salvia officinalis
SAGE

Among the most widely grown and popular herbs, sage is a spreading, evergreen shrub seldom more than 2 ft (60 cm) in height. Its finely wrinkled, gray-green leaves are decorative, as are the tubular, two-lipped, purple flowers that appear in summer. It is a native of stony hillsides in southern Europe and it has given rise to several variegated leaved cultivars, including *S.o.* 'Aurea', *S.o.* 'Tricolor' and the purple-leaved *S.o.* 'Purpurascens'.

Propagation *Cuttings taken in spring or late summer root easily. In mild winter areas, hardwood cuttings can be inserted on site. Sow seed under cover in late winter or outside in spring.*

Soil *A well-drained soil is needed; poor, sandy or limy soil is acceptable, though one of moderate fertility is better.*

Position *A site in sun with good air circulation is the best but a little morning or afternoon shade is tolerated.*

Cultivation *Set young plants in their permanent sites in spring. In severe winter areas, rooted cuttings or plants must be overwintered under cover.*

An easy way to prepare sage leaves for storing is to make a wooden slatted tray or one covered with chicken wire. Pick sprigs of leaves as soon as they reach full size, lay them thinly on the tray and place it in an airing cupboard or over a radiator. In the latter case, make sure the leaves are out of direct sun while they dry off.

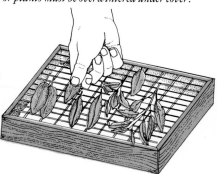

Salvia Sclarea
CLARY

This plant is a short-lived perennial to about 3 ft (90 cm) tall. The large, oval base leaves are downy and wrinkled, the upper ones smaller, and accompanying spikes of tubular lilac flowers are surrounded by white, pink or purple-tinted bracts.

Propagation *Seed is the usual means of increase, sown in nursery rows in late spring.*
Soil *Moderately fertile soil that does not dry out too rapidly is the ideal.*
Position *A sunny site is best but some shade is tolerated, especially in hot summer areas.*
Cultivation *Young plants should be set out in permanent sites in fall, spacing them about 1½ ft (45 cm) apart. If leaves only are required, the flowering stems must be pinched out when young. This will prolong the life of the plant. If flowering takes place, it is best to treat clary as a biennial.*

Vigorous young leaves are the part of this herb used for flavoring. To foster their production, pinch out the flower spikes as soon as they appear and certainly before flowers expand. Water freely during dry spells and apply a high nitrogen fertilizer if growth slows down.

Sambucus nigra
ELDER

Common or European elder (*Sambucus nigra*) and the sweet American elder (*S. canadensis*) are seldom grown for their herbal uses now, although flowers can be used to make elder champagne and the berries a red wine. There are cultivated varieties, selected for the size and flavor of their fruits. Others have ornamental variegated foliage. These elders are large shrubs with pinnate leaves, large flat heads of white flowers in summer and glossy black berries.

Propagation *Take hardwood cuttings and plant them on site or in a nursery plot in fall.*
Soil *Any fertile, moist but not wet soil is suitable.*
Position *Sun and partial shade are equally satisfactory, though growth will be taller and thinner in shade.*
Cultivation *Set out young plants in their permanent sites in fall or spring and in mild areas throughout the winter. Cultivars grown for their variegated foliage should be hard pruned annually in late winter or early spring.*

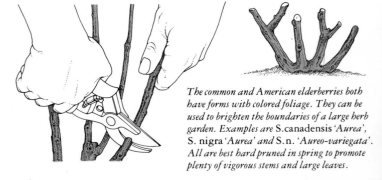

The common and American elderberries both have forms with colored foliage. They can be used to brighten the boundaries of a large herb garden. Examples are S.canadensis 'Aurea', S. nigra 'Aurea' and S.n. 'Aureo-variegata'. All are best hard pruned in spring to promote plenty of vigorous stems and large leaves.

Santolina Chamaecyparissus
LAVENDER COTTON

This plant is a bright foliaged, low shrub from western and central Mediterranean regions. It forms a dense mound to 2 ft (60 cm) high and often wider, with silvery-gray, slender, rather mossy foliage. In summer, branched clusters of button-like, yellow flower-heads appear. Lavender cotton is now primarily grown as an aromatic, ornamental foliage plant.

Propagation *Take cuttings in late summer and keep the young plants under cover during the winter months.*

Soil *A well-drained soil is essential, ideally of only moderate fertility. Rich soils promote soft, floppy growth.*

Position *A sunny site is needed to keep the plants compact and decorative.*

Cultivation *Put young plants in their positions in spring. If a purely foliage effect is required, the flowering stems must be cut off when young. Where temperatures drop to 5°F (−15°C) or below, plants are best overwintered under cover or protected on site.*

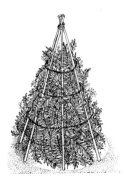

The simplest way to protect lavender cotton in winter is to make a tripod of canes over the plant, then cover them during cold spells with spruce branches (left) or plastic sheeting. More efficient is a collar made from a sandwich of chicken wire with a 4–5 in (10–15 cm) filling of bracken or straw (right).

Satureja hortensis
SUMMER SAVORY

Summer savory has been used as a flavoring herb since at least Roman times. It is a slender, erect annual 6–12 in (15–30 cm) or so in height, with wiry stems and narrow leaves to ¾ in (2 cm) long. Terminal leafy spikes of small lavender or white flowers open in late summer. Fresh, finely chopped leaves can be added to cheese and egg dishes and used to make a white sauce to accompany beans.

Propagation *Seed is the only means of increase and should be sown thinly on site in spring.*
Soil *Well-drained soil is essential, ideally of moderate fertility but not rich.*
Position *A location in sun is the ideal.*
Cultivation *Seedlings must be thinned with care to achieve a final spacing of 6 in (15 cm) apart. Weeding must be regularly attended to during these early stages and water given in dry spells. For storing, cut the stems when the first flowers open and hang to dry in a shady, airy place.*

If a winter supply of summer savory is wanted, it must be dried when summer growth is at its best. Just as flowering begins, cut leafy shoots 9–12 in (24–30 cm) long (left). Tie in small bunches and hang, heads downward, in a warm, airy place (right).

Satureja montana
WINTER SAVORY

Though closely related to summer savory, this is an evergreen sub-shrub to 1 ft (30 cm) or more tall, with leaves to 1 in (2.5 cm) long and pale, rose-purple, pinkish or white flowers. The flavor of the leaves is milder than those of summer savory but it has more culinary uses.

Propagation *Division in spring or cuttings in summer are both easy means of increase. Alternatively, sow seed on site in spring.*
Soil *A well-drained soil is essential, ideally of moderate fertility but quite poor soil is acceptable.*
Position *A sunny site is needed, though half-day shade is tolerated.*
Cultivation *Set out young plants in their permanent quarters in spring, or in fall in mild winter areas, spacing them 1 ft (30 cm) apart. Harvest in the same way as for summer savory.*

The best way to increase winter savory is by cuttings in late summer. Remove non-flowering lateral shoots, trim to 2–3 in (5–7.5 cm) in length and insert around the edge of a pot of sandy soil; then keep it in warm, humid conditions (right). When rooted, pot singly and overwinter under cover (far right). Plant out the following spring.

Sesamum indicum
SESAME

This tropical herb is seldom cultivated outside in cool summer areas. It is an annual to 2 ft (60 cm) or more, with erect stems and lance-shaped leaves 2½–5 in (6–13 cm) long. The stem tips terminate in leafy spikes of tubular, pale pink to white flowers about 1 in (2.5 cm) long. The mildly aromatic seeds are used in bakery and also yield benne (gingili) oil, used medicinally and for cooking.

Propagation *Seed is the only means of increase, sown at 70–75°F (21–24°C) in early spring. The seedlings are best pricked off into 3 in (7.5 cm) pots.*

Soil *A fertile soil, preferably enriched with organic matter, moist but well drained, is the ideal.*

Position *A sunny and wind-sheltered location is needed. In cool summer areas, sesame is best grown in pots under glass.*

Cultivation *Young plants must not be set outside until all fear of frost has passed. Once the seed pods ripen and begin to split, the stems, with pods attached, must be cut and put in a warm, airy place.*

Sesame seeds need warmth to germinate and grow successfully. Sow seed in pots, pans or boxes (right), depending on the number of plants required. As soon as the seedlings show their first true or rough leaves, pot singly in 3 in (7.5 cm) containers of good quality potting mix (far right).

Symphytum officinale
COMFREY

This is a robust, clump-forming perennial to 2 ft (60 cm) or more, with big, pointed, oval basal leaves. The branched stems bear smaller leaves and nodding clusters of tubular ½ in (1 cm) long, off-white, purple or yellowish flowers in summer. Similar, but more robust and with purple-flowers, is *S. × uplandicum*, the Russian comfrey. Comfrey is essentially a medicinal herb to promote healing.

Propagation *Division of established clumps in fall or spring is the usual means of increase. Alternatively, sow seeds in nursery rows when ripe.*
Soil *Moist soil is essential for vigorous growth though ordinary soil gives adequate results.*
Position *Sun or partial shade is equally acceptable. In drier soils some shade is advisable, especially in the middle part of the day.*
Cultivation *Young plants should be set out in their permanent sites in fall or spring. In drier sites, watering is necessary.*

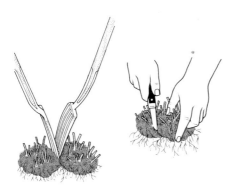

Comfrey is propagated by division though a big, old plant may be tough. Dig up the clump, thrust two forks back to back in the middle and pry apart (far right).

If the two-fork method is not easy, use a pruning knife (left) or sharp spade. Break up each clump into individual crowns and plant immediately.

Tanacetum vulgare
TANSY

A lso most aptly known as golden-buttons, tansy is a widely clump-forming plant 2–3 ft (60–90 cm) tall. The rich green, ferny leaves and clusters of button-like yellow flower heads are decorative. Leaves can be used in moderation as a flavoring herb.

Propagation *Division of established clumps in spring is the usual method.*
Soil *Almost any soil is suitable, though one of moderate fertility is best.*
Position *The sturdiest plants develop in full sun but partial shade is tolerated.*
Cultivation *Set out young plants in their permanent sites in fall or spring. When established, each plant can spread vigorously; lift and divide every two or three years, retaining only the healthiest pieces.*

Many herbs are raised in pots. Before planting out, water well, allow to drain, then remove the plant by upending the container and rapping the rim on a wooden bench.

Dig a hole with a trowel, making it larger than the root ball of the plant. Position the plant, fill the gaps with soil and firm with the fists.

As the firming is completed, leave a shallow depression around the plant to facilitate watering. Unless the soil is thoroughly moist, complete the operation with a good watering.

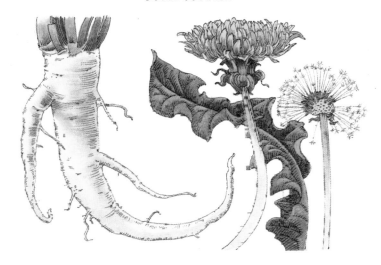

Taraxacum officinale
DANDELION

It has often been said that if the dandelion were a rare plant it would be much sought after by gardeners. It has shapely, bright yellow flower heads and boldly toothed, rich green leaves that grow in a rosette. The flowers make an excellent wine and the dried and ground roots are a chicory substitute. Leaves can be blanched for winter salads and spring leaves eaten like spinach. Robust cultivars are available commercially.

Propagation *Sow seed thinly on site in spring.*
Soil *Almost any soil that is not very dry is suitable, but for fat roots and juicy leaves a fertile, moist but not wet soil is needed.*
Position *Sunny or partially shady positions are equally acceptable.*
Cultivation *Young plants should be thinned to about 10 in (25 cm) apart and kept watered in dry weather. For a winter crop, the roots must be lifted in batches from early winter onward, the leaves removed and the roots packed in boxes of soil or peat. They must then be kept dark at a medium temperature of 55–60°F (10–13°C).*

For winter salads, dig up specially grown dandelions about six weeks before use. Cut off the leaves ½ in (1 cm) above the crown and discard them (above). Trim the roots to 6 in (15 cm), pack vertically in containers of soil and keep in the dark (right).

Teucrium Chamaedrys
GERMANDER

This herb is suitable in the flower garden. It is a shrubby evergreen perennial to about 1 ft (30 cm) in height. The small, dark green leaves are oval to oblong and strongly toothed. In late summer, whorled spikes of small, rose-purple flowers expand. Each blossom is tubular, about ½ in (1 cm) long, with a gaping mouth and a large, rounded lower lip. It is included in *pot-pourris* but formerly was used as a tonic.

Propagation *Take cuttings in summer; alternatively, divide clumps or sow seed in spring.*

Soil *A well-drained soil is essential but apart from this almost any soil is suitable. Even dryish, sandy or limy soil is tolerated.*

Position *A sunny place is best but up to half-day shade is tolerated.*

Cultivation *Set out young plants in their permanent sites in spring, or fall in mild winter areas. Shear them over after flowering.*

Germander is usually increased by cuttings in late summer. Remove non-flowering stems and trim to about 3 in (7.5 cm) long, cutting above and below a pair of leaves.

Dip the cut stem ends in a rooting powder containing a fungicide.

Place several cuttings around the edge of a 3 in (7.5 cm) pot of sandy soil. When rooted, pot-on singly into 3 in (7.5 cm) pots and overwinter under cover.

Thymus × *citriodora*
LEMON THYME

Lemon thyme is a hybrid between garden thyme (*T. vulgaris*) and the larger wild thyme, *T. pulegioides*. It is similar in habit and size to common thyme but the leaves, rich green and lemon scented, are preferable for stuffings. Larger wild thyme is a prostrate, mat-forming plant with a scent similar to that of common thyme.

Propagation *Divide or layer in spring, or take cuttings in late summer.*
Soil *Sandy or limy, sharply-drained soil is essential. Rich soil will produce uncharacteristic growth.*
Position *A sunny position is needed, though a little shade is tolerated.*
Cultivation *Young plants can be put in their permanent sites in spring or, in areas of mild winters, in fall. Where winters are long and severe, protect plants or keep them in containers under cover. To maintain compact growth, shear off the flowering stems annually when they have faded.*

Lemon, caraway and garden thymes can make small, fragrant lawns. Mowing to remove the spent flowering stems is seldom necessary more than once a year. Cut small areas with hedging shears.

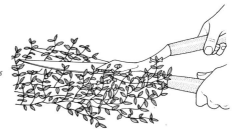

Thymus Herba-barona
CARAWAY THYME

Caraway-scented thyme is a sprawling, mat-forming plant up to, but usually less than, 4 in (10 cm) tall. The evergreen leaves are variably hairy up to ½ in (1 cm) in length. The pale purple flowers are ½ in (1 cm) long and carried in terminal heads in summer. The scent is strong and the herb was used to flavor bacon or beef and steaks. It can also be used in stuffings and *bouquet garni*. *Thymus caespititius* is more likely to be seen in a rock garden or alpine house than the herb garden. It forms compact cushions, ultimately 10 in (25 cm) or more tall, with narrow, hairy-margined leaves and dense, rounded heads of pink or purple flowers. In its Mediterranean homeland it yields a volatile oil used in medicines and perfumery. It is attractive to bees.

Propagation *Sow seed under cover or divide in spring. Take cuttings in late summer and overwinter in a frame.*
Soil *Well-drained, alkaline or sandy soil is needed of average fertility.*
Position *A sunny location is necessary, though a little morning or afternoon shade is acceptable.*
Cultivation *Place young plants in their permanent positions in spring or, in mild winter areas, early fall. Where winters are severe, the plants are best grown in containers and kept under cover. To maintain compact plants, shear them annually after flowering.*

Thymus vulgaris
GARDEN THYME

Garden or common thyme is an evergreen shrub, native to the western Mediterranean region. Wiry-stemmed and of bushy habit, it grows 8–12 in (20–30 cm) in height and has a spread of up to twice as much. The small, grayish leaves are up to ⅓ in (8 mm) in length and make an effective background for the profusely borne heads of tiny pink to lilac flowers in summer. It has long been used in cooking and its leaves have antiseptic properties.

Propagation *Divide or layer in spring. Alternatively, sow seed at the same time, preferably under cover, or root cuttings in late summer.*
Soil *Ordinary to quite poor soil is suitable but it must be well drained.*
Position *A sunny location is essential, though a little morning or afternoon shade is tolerated.*
Cultivation *Young plants are best set out in their permanent sites in spring. In areas of severe winters, protection is necessary. Alternatively, plants can be grown in containers and brought on under cover in fall.*

Thyme can make an attractive ground-cover plant but unless it is controlled, growth will become leggy. Maintain compact, healthy plants by cutting off the flowering stems after flowers have faded. Even with care, plants may begin to lose their attractiveness after a few years. They are best replaced with young specimens.

TROPAEOLACEAE

Tropaeolum majus
NASTURTIUM

The alternative vernacular name, Bitter Indian, is as confusing as nasturtium for this plant, *Nasturtium* being the scientific name of watercress. Long grown for its ornamental value, this plant is seldom thought of as a herb but all parts of the plant are edible. Normally a climber or trailer with stems 6½– 10 ft (2–3 m) in length, the dwarf 'Gleam' sort is best for the herb garden.

Propagation *Seed is the usual means of increase. Sow either on site when frosts cease or earlier under cover.*
Soil *Any moderately fertile, well-drained but not dry soil is suitable.*
Position *A sunny site is best but half-day shade is tolerated.*
Cultivation *Young plants raised early under cover must not be set outside until all fear of frost has passed. A support of strings, wire or trellis must be provided for the climbing cultivars. If used as a trailer, plenty of hanging room is needed.*

Garden nasturtium makes a splendid summer screen at the edge of a patio or to divide the vegetable plot from the rest of the garden. Use trellis secured to strong stakes in a design of your choice as a support (above).

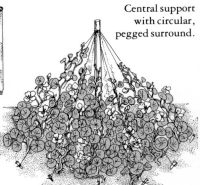

Central support with circular, pegged surround.

Glossary

Words in *italic* type denote other Glossary entries.

Annual A plant that grows from seed, flowers, produces seed and dies within the space of a single growing season. Compare *Biennial* and *Perennial*.

Biennial A plant that grows from seed, flowers, produces seed and dies within the space of two growing seasons. Compare *Annual* and *Perennial*.

Coldframe Any type of covered frame that admits light and protects plants but is unheated.

Deciduous Term applied to those plants that lose their leaves in winter, when they become dormant and almost all growth ceases. Compare *Evergreen*.

Drill Narrow, usually shallow furrow made in the soil for planting seeds.

Evergreen Said of plants that retain their leaves throughout the year. Compare *Deciduous*.

Flat A lidless box, which can be of various shapes but is usually oblong, used for planting seeds.

Growing tip The uppermost tip of a stem, where growth is usual.

Hardwood Mature shoots from which cuttings are taken for propagation. Compare *Semi-hardwood* and *Softwood*.

Knot garden Arrangement of plants, especially herbs, in a pattern resembling that which might be made by a knot of rope. Knot gardens, of 15th-century origin, were designed to be seen from above, usually from a window or terrace.

Mulch Organic matter, such as straw, grass cuttings and peat, applied as a *top dressing* around plants to provide additional nourishment and to suppress weeds.

Nursery row (Nursery bed) A garden area used for rearing young plants before they are transplanted to their permanent sites.

Perennial A plant that lives for at least three seasons, usually many more. Compare *Annual* and *Biennial*.

Pinching out Removal of the *growing tip* of a plant, usually undertaken to encourage development of side shoots.

Rhizome A fleshy stem that acts as a storage organ, lasting for more than one growing season and usually horizontal and underground.

Semi-hardwood Shoots just starting to harden at the base, taken for propagation. Compare *Hardwood* and *Softwood*.

Softwood Young, soft shoots of woody plants from which cuttings are taken for propagation. Compare *Hardwood* and *Semi-hardwood*.

Tilth Finely broken down soil, produced by good cultivation.

Top dressing Term used to describe artificial fertilizer, lime, sand or other concentrated substance, when applied to the soil without cultivation. Compare *Mulch*.

Index

Acknowledgments

Dorling Kindersley would like to thank Alison Chappel for her special assistance and the following artists for the illustrations: David Ashby, Will Giles, Vana Haggerty, Vanessa Luff, Peter Morter, Coral Mula, Donald Myall, Sandra Pond, Rodney Shackell and Eric Thomas.

Typesetting

D. P. Media, Hitchin, U.K.

Reproduction

Repro Llovet, Barcelona, Spain.